Facebook Marketing

----- ❧❧❧❧ -----

A Comprehensive Guide for Building Authority, Creating Engagement and Making Money Through Facebook

Mark Smith

Table of Contents

Additionally, the information in the following pages is intended only for informational purposes and should thus be thought of as universal. As befitting its nature, it is presented without assurance regarding its prolonged validity or interim quality. Trademarks that are mentioned are done without written consent and can in no way be considered an endorsement from the trademark holder.

Introduction

Congratulations on downloading your personal copy of *Facebook Marketing: A Comprehensive Guide for Building Authority, Creating Engagement and Making Money through Facebook.* Thank you for doing so.

The following chapters will discuss some of the basics that you need to know in order to get started with Facebook marketing. It is one of the best marketing options that you can use to really form a relationship with your customers and promote your business. This book is going to spend some time talking about how to get started and will offer tips, proven strategies, and wisdom nuggets for building a powerful and profitable Facebook business.

The techniques shared in this book will be as straightforward and actionable as possible so even beginners can get their feet wet in the lucrative world of Facebook marketing.

There are plenty of books on this subject on the market, thanks again for choosing this one! Every effort was made to ensure it is full of as much useful information as possible, please enjoy!

Chapter One:

Introduction to Facebook Marketing

Did you know that about 1.09 billion internet users log in to Facebook daily, with the number growing at a staggering 16% each year? It is one of the most popular social media platforms that account for 77% of all social media logins. Little wonder, then, those millions of ambitious online entrepreneurs are tapping into this beehive of viral activity related to both- personal and business accounts.

According to a Quicksprout survey, 80% of social media users in the United States prefer connecting with brands via Facebook.

Facebook is a brilliant medium for engaging visitors, building authority, driving traffic to your website and increasing your credibility as a brand. It helps you laser target your audience, and convert these interested people into leads, ultimately creating a base of loyal customers. Thus any business can leverage the power of Facebook to boost engagement, optimize their presence and build a solid brand.

Yes, it can be challenging to master the nuances of social media as it's a dynamic platform that keeps adding, deleting and modifying features. However, once you progress through the learning curve, your business can benefit tremendously from the power of a buzzing Facebook page.

Think of it this way. You've recently met a woman/man you fancy, and would love to spend the rest of your life with them. What would be your best approach? Befriend them. Get to know more about their likes and dislikes, while striking a meaningful friendship based on common goals and interests. You may ask them out for coffee initially, build a rapport, and then do long dinner-movie dates. Eventually, you may pop the question, and spend the rest of your life with the man/woman you really dig.

What do you think would've happened if you would have simply walked up to them on seeing them for the first time and popped the question? Chances are they would've thought you are nuts, and simply scooted in the opposite direction to never see you again in this lifetime. A perfectly wonderful chance ruined.

This pretty much sums up how the social media works too, and why it is such a brilliant platform for increasing your chances of success. It helps you build a rapport with potential customers through engagement and conversation. You can't simply launch a business and expect people to queue up for buying. Any astute business person will realize that the customers buy from brands and people they love. People have got to love you and your brand to be able to relate to it and buy from you. This can be super effectively accomplished through engagement, conversation and constant communication with potential customers.

Social media marketing isn't different from dating. You're wooing your customers through engagement, making your brand appealing, offering value to potential buyers, and finally turning them into lifelong buyers. Facebook helps you create a strong base of loyal customers who act as your brand evangelists. They help spread a good word about your products or services within their social circle.

Did you ever move countries or cities? What was it like? A bit of culture shock? Of course, it can be perplexing to a new language, diverse people, and a different culture. You need to know about the accepted norms to fit in or learn about local customs and behavior before you gain the complete trust of locals.

This is how Facebook or any social media platforms works too. There are spoken and unspoken rules of the game that you must learn to adhere to if you want to build a desirable brand and profitable business.

One of the biggest advantages of using Facebook for your business is that it's a highly versatile platform that can be channelized to achieve multiple business goals. Your business goals can be anything from increasing conversions to building authority to boosting engagement. With its multiple tools, resources, and functions, Facebook can you achieve virtually any business goal.

Think of it as an online counterpart of a water cooler or an erstwhile town square. People collect near a water cooler (or town square in earlier times) and discuss just anything they fancy that brings them together. They share jaw dropping details about the latest breaking news or Game of Thrones episode while forging strong connections over shared conversation. It gets so interesting that they actually look forward to the next informal, engaging meeting at the designated spot.

If you've attended a cocktail party where you barely know anyone, you're doing pretty much a live version of what social media or Facebook marketing entails. You try to spot people who might be interested in you or who you share common interests with. There is a preliminary introduction where you get to know people. You crack jokes, build a connection by engaging others, have a meaningful conversation, and eventually promised to stay in touch with people. If you are interesting and authoritative, people will remember you (brand building) and look forward to meeting you again.

Facebook is an online cocktail party, where brands and customers are getting to know, and benefitting each other. When you post interesting and valuable stuff that your audience appreciates, people like your brand. They find it familiar and appealing, and establish a connection, which eventually helps when it comes to making a purchasing decision. Facebook is not merely a platform for selling (though it serves this purpose well too), it is also a powerful resource for building relationships.

Let's take two newly launched brands of soaps. Soap A barely has a social media or Facebook presence. They channelize all their resources print and billboard ads, hoping to make their brand familiar and desirable among their target audience.

Soap B, on the other hand, has a powerful Facebook presence. It posts thoroughly researched, easy to share, interesting and valuable information related to hygiene, skin care, and beauty.

Their target audience loves to share the posts the Brand B because it makes them look really smart and well-informed within their social circle. The brand's page is abuzz with activity, with people sharing lots of information. If people are given a choice between

Brand A and Brand B on a supermarket shelf, which brand do you think they are likelier to pick? Brand B will have a more engaged audience, which may make its recall and recognition value higher. People can relate to Brand B on a more personal level because it has made an effort to establish personal connections with its target audience. This is the true power of social media, which can be used to grow a variety of businesses.

You'll learn some of the best Facebook marketing strategies right here, which have the potential to skyrocket your business. Hop aboard, and get ready for the adventure of a lifetime!

Chapter Two:

Facebook Marketing Tips for Beginners

Here are some highly proven and effective Facebook marketing tips to keep you ahead in the learning curve if you are just getting started with the seemingly big bag world of social media marketing.

1. Build a Business Profile

It's astounding how many people make this faux pas and lose out in the bargain. As a basic thumb rule, never ever do business through a personal profile. Build a distinct business profile page that effectively represents a brand. These pages don't appear too different from personal profiles but have a series of tools through which your audience can endorse your brand by liking the page, viewing regular updates, and commenting on your posts.

Creating a distinct brand page maximizes your business's chances of reaching out to a large number of interested customers. Also, it is against Facebook's Service Terms and Conditions to use personal profiles for anything other than personal interactions.

Also, if you've created a personal profile page for your brand or business, you should consider converting it into a business page. This way you'll still retain your personal account, while simultaneously having a business page.

Keep in mind that a profile can be converted into a business page just once. Once you've converted the personal account into a business, Facebook transfers your profile picture along with the cover picture to the new page. The page's name on the personal account becomes its business page name. Facebook offers tons of features that help move information from the personal profile page to a business page (takes 14 days from the date of conversion).

Choose friends from your personal profile to like your page automatically; however, posts on your personal profile will not be transferred to the new business page. The business page can also be managed via your personal account.

to convert your personal account into a Facebook business page:

1. Click on https://www.facebook.com/pages/create/migrate

2. Next, go to the "Get Started" button and follow all instructions to successfully migrate a personal business profile into a proper Facebook business page.

Having a business page offers me you multiple advantages, including the opportunity to laser target customers through Facebook's paid promotion feature and the ability to create events.

2. Create an Appealing and Memorable Vanity URL

Yes, the social media is as much about visual brilliance as it's about content and substance. Vain as it sounds, your page has to look gorgeous to pique the curiosity of people enough to come and explore it.

Once you've built a business page, Facebook assigns a random number to the URL, which means your page looks something like

facebook.com/pages/businessname/2346578.

A pro tip if you want to increase your page's shareable value or make it easy to find is to create a more identifiable, appealing, and memorable URL such as

Facebook.com/Sunshineflorists.

Go to General Account Settings, and change your URL into a more recognizable page name from the Username option.

3. Add a Recognizable and Attention Grabbing Cover Photo

Next, add a stunning cover photo to create a desirable visual effect. Facebook allows 851 x 315-pixel cover images right at the top of your business page. Optimize your cover photo to grab the attention of your target audience, hook them enough to explore more about your products/services, and offer an efficient mobile browsing experience.

Your cover photo is the first thing people spot when they visit your page because it occupies considerable space, and strategically sits right at the top of the page. Here are some tips to keep in mind to optimize the appeal for your Facebook cover photo.

1. This seems like a given, but it's still not funny how many people actually overlook it. Follow Facebook's guidelines when it comes to creating a cover photo because it's just not the smartest thing to lose your page for a cover photo guideline violation.

    Read the full terms and conditions before you go about uploading a cover photo for the business page. In general keep in mind that your cover image is public. Don't make it misleading, irrelevant or deceptive. Also, don't infringe someone else's copyright simply by lifting images from various sources.

2. Ensure that the image is optimized to the right size and resolution. It should be 828 x 315 px on a desktop interface, and 640 x 360 px tall on a mobile interface. Make sure you get these dimensions right while designing the photo, otherwise you'll keep tweaking it while uploading the image. Design anything smaller than this, and Facebook will end up stretching the image, making it look unprofessional and tacky. To make your task easier, you can simply download a pre-sized Facebook cover photo template with a simple Google search.

3. The placement of profile pictures on Facebook makes it tough to view a section of the cover photo unless it's clicked on. In addition to the profile picture, the page name and buttons also hide a section of the cover photo. Keep this in mind and don't include important pieces of imagery or content in these portions, which aren't immediately visible or viewable to users.

Since Facebook positions your profile picture on the left, it is a good strategy to right align your cover photograph to maintain a balance, and make your brand/product clearly visible, while also appearing more aesthetically elegant. You will be able to attract greater focus to the brand or product by right aligning your Facebook cover image.

Ensure the photo is visible for mobile viewing since more than half of your user base will view your page from handheld devices. Compared to the desktop, a larger portion of your cover page is hidden by the profile picture. The page name also appears on the cover photo, which impacts its visibility. Keep all this in mind before designing your cover photo.

4. Try incorporating your Facebook cover photo with other design elements on the page to maintain consistency and uniformity in your brand's visual identity. If the dominant colors in your logo are red and yellow, stick a cover photo where red and yellow are prominently displayed. Don't see it as an isolated or individual design element. Rather make the cover photo a part of a larger overall canvas that balances multiple design elements to draw optimal attention on your Facebook page.

Some of the best business pages combine their cover photo and profile picture and make it look integrated, like two sections of a single brand canvas. This is a subtle, yet compelling way to conveying your brand identity.

4. Add an Awesome Profile Picture

Facebook allows you to upload a recognizable profile picture such as a company logo image of your products/services or a headshot if you are a solo entrepreneur. If you want your target audience to find and like your page, choose your profile image smartly. Keep in mind that it is also displayed as a thumbnail image next to every update.

The dimensions of a Facebook profile photo are 180 x 180 px (160 x 160 px on desktop machines).

5. Optimize The About Section

When people need more information about your brand/business, they are most likely to browse through the "About" section of your page.

Ensure the page is optimized for social media and search engines by including a detailed and impactful description of your business using the most relevant keywords that define the enterprise/brand. Give visitors a good feel of what the page is about in the opening lines of your description. A brief section of the detailed "About" description will be extracted and displayed under "Short Description by Facebook.

Include as many details as possible that visitors may find useful in your "About" section, including a phone number, physical address (if required), website URL, email, business opening hours, price range, a link to your product and service catalog and other relevant information.

6. Earn The Very Responsive Badge

One of the first things you must aim to accomplish after creating a business page is earning a "very responsive to messages" Facebook awards pages who have a response percentage of 90% and a response time of less than 15 minutes over a period of one week.

Having this badge makes customers view you as a prompt, communicative and reliable business which makes an effort to connect with customers. It shows you are tuned into your audience's queries and care enough to offer them a speedy response. Even if you can't give an immediate solution to the customer, try and keep your response time high by replying and letting them know that you will get back to them with a solution as soon as you've figured it out. It makes you come across as professional, friendly and concerned.

7. Include Milestones

Use the "Milestones" feature on Facebook to highlight your brand's most notable achievements. Events you can include under the milestone feature are the year your brand/business was launched, awards it won in the past, product releases and other noteworthy accolades.

Users will find your brand more credible and authoritative when you display your accomplishments. Basically, a great way to blow your own trumpet and keep customers in the loop about your brand's evolution.

8. Call to Action

Facebook has included in what is being hailed as one its best business page features. It allows visitors to place easy, visible, and effective call to action buttons on their page. Select from one of the pre-defined call to action buttons such as "contact us", "book now", "sign up", "use app" and more. This is a great tool for linking the relevant website page or landing page with your Facebook business page.

How to Add a CTA button to Your Facebook Business Page

Log in and go to your Facebook Business page.

Click on the "Call to Action" button positioned on top of the page next to the Like button.

It's no rocket science really. Make it easy for your customers to do what you want them to do by telling them what they're supposed to do.

9. Create Unique Page Tabs

Facebook offers a set of predefined page tabs such as About, Photos, Likes and other similar options. However, you can also create custom tabs that can perform functions similar to landing pages within the business page. The tabs are located at the top of your business page. For example, if you want to invite entries for a draw or competition, create a custom "enter competition" or "submit your entry" tab for the purpose. Link it to the submit entries page on your website.

How to Create Unique Page Tabs?

Sign in to your business page. Select the "More" tab.

Next, select the Manage Tabs option from a dropdown list.

10. Post Best Blog Content

Most businesses rely on social media to offer their target audience a steady stream of valuable and interesting content. Avoid populating the timeline with every blog post. Cherry pick only the best ones that are entertaining, useful, relevant and informative.

Several blogging platforms offer a feature where the software automatically updates each new blog postand publishes it on your page. All you need to do this sync your blog page with your Facebook business page, and auto-publish content. However, it's best to publish content that will engage interested fans, and keep them hooked.

Also, each time you post a blog link on Facebook, the page pulls a short description along with an image. This description is extracted from your blog page's meta description (the description that is specifically created to show up as the page's description on the search engine results page preview). Ensure your meta description is relevant, accurate and well-written.

without a properly written meta description, Facebook will simply pull out anything it finds without the relevant keywords and phrases, which is a huge lost opportunity. It will hamper the overall user experience, and fail to attract customers to your business.

Sum up your posts in under 155 characters by drafting a power-packed meta description. Don't waste your valuable space real estate in including preposterously long links to the post within the post. The thumbnail URL is enough to send readers to your blog post. Use your space wisely for piquing the reader's curiosity or grabbing their attention.

Many newbie marketers misleadingly believe that posting frequently increases the visibility of their posts. Facebook's algorithms aren't as straightforward. It all boils down to the quality of posts, and the engagement it attracts. Posting more frequently won't help you reach more people unless you are targeting people in different time zones and have a clear objective for posting frequently.

Poor quality posts that receive little response end up affecting your statistics, and can even go on to reduce your visibility among your followers. Facebook has slick practices in place to filter out low-quality and irrelevant posts. Put up top quality posts only, and watch your numbers soar.

Give importance to quality over quantity by being selective about your posts. Don't overwhelm your target audience by drafting multiple posts. Rather, take the time to create delightful posts that your audience will love to share within their social circle.

Adorn your posts with high-quality visuals and videos to increase their appeal. Facebook posts with interesting and relevant visuals witness 2.3x greater engagement than imageless posts.

Even if you have a blog with several posts, optimize it for Facebook by adding new videos and slick images. Any fool-proof social media or Facebook strategy includes images, videos, infographics, tables, charts and screenshots that offer tremendous value to your audience.

Follow the 80-20 social media thumb rule, where 80 percent of your posts are dedicated to non-promotional posts (aimed at increasing engagement and establishing connections), while 20 percent posts are channelized towards directly promoting your products or services.

People don't really fancy being sold to on social media. They view it more as a platform for discussion, communication and forging connections. Therefore, your social media strategy needs to be subtle and more directed towards building a brand and making connections, which eventually turn into loyal customers.

11. Focus On Offering Value

As any internet or social media marketer will tell you, you must give value first to receive business from your customers later. Initially, the focus is only on building connections, credibility, and authority. Don't focus on hard selling in the early stages of your business.

For instance, if you run an organic products e-store, the standard marketing strategy would be to post images of your products and urge customers to buy them. However, this isn't how Facebook or social media marketing works.

Instead of hard selling your products, create blog posts about healthy, organic recipes using ingredients you sell. Share links of the recipes on your page. At the bottom of these recipes, subtly mention that these products can be easily sourced from your website.

In the above example, ensure your content strategy includes a variety of recipes catering to conscious eaters or health buffs such as "20 Easy to Make and Healthy Lunch Box Recipes For Kids" or "Simple and Healthy Smoothies for Diabetics" or "15 Healthy and Delicious One Pot Organic Meals." Do you get the drift?

Oreo's Facebook page is crazy popular because they connect with their fans by offering them tons of delicious, innovative and fun Oreo recipes, complemented by tempting images.

They also use a bunch of clever and appealing hashtags. Who can resist?

Social media users lap up content that has high utility or informational value. They also love to share content that makes them look really smart among their friends. Post high-value, intelligently written and useful content, and people will be more than happy to spread the word.

Dove is another brand that has its social media strategy brilliantly figured out. They created a video a couple of years back, which earned them thousands of likes and about half a million views. The brand was barely mentioned in the video. Dove was simply focused on telling stories that evoke emotions and make their relatable.

They told stories about everyday women and encouraged their fans to tag women who inspired them, thus helping the brand get its word out without aggressively marketing their products. Women found these stories relatable and connected with the brand on an emotional, nostalgic level.

12. Images

Did you know that Facebook posts with images receive 84 percent higher link clicks than those with visuals? It's simple. Present people with stuff that looks stunning, is easy to understand and evokes some emotion.

Tell stories through pictures. It's called humanizing your brand. People love behind the scenes stories about businesses and brands. They like to think that they are dealing with real people who care about them and not factory bots.

Create everyday slice of life or behind the scenes posts about your business. Introduce your customers to your employees.

Give them a peek about how the products they use are actually created.

Pictures of real people help people connect with your brand. While using images for Facebook posts, focus on people's faces. Facial profile images work well for Facebook posts.

Rather than using images of the product, include lifestyle images. You need to tap into your audience's aspirations by showing them the lifestyle your product/service represents. Use images that induce a strong sense of nostalgia. Make image galleries and collages if you want to share multiple images to make it easy for your audience to access all images in a single postrather than creating multiple, confusing posts.

Use bright, high resolution and eye-catching images. Low-lit images with dull colors don't receive much traction on the social media.

Well, people may say they are annoyed with constantly seeing pictures of where their friends are dining or what they are up to. However, the fact is, they are still viewing it. According to Social Media Examiner, images make up for 87 percent of the content shared on Facebook.

Just browse through a few business pages, and you'll discover how a majority of them use stock photos rather than original images. Use real, natural photographs rather than generic stock images. Posts that have original, real pictures come across as more relatable and organic.

Another smart tip is to integrate your Instagram images in your Facebook feed.

Tap on the settings option in your Instagram account, and link your Facebook account. Every Time you take a picture, tap on the Facebook icon for sharing those pictures on your Facebook news feed.

13. Make Content Easy to Share

It is a golden nugget of wisdom in internet marketing circles that if you make anything too complicated for your audience, they are less likely to do it. This explains all the spoon-feeding (click here, visit our page, buy now etc. links).

People generally have less time and a shorter attention span when they are browsing the internet. They won't spend time trying to figure out things if it looks complicated or if they don't know what action to take.

Make sharing your posts a cakewalk for them by using prominent "Share" or "Like" buttons on your blog page. Use the Facebook Follow button to increase your reach. People can like your page with a single click, while also viewing the total number of likes received by the page. This sort of validates your page or offers social proof to prospective and existing customers.

Adding Facebook social share buttons encourages your web audience to connect and communicate with your brand on Facebook, while also increasing the reach of your content by sharing it.

with the Facebook Like Box, visitors can view your follower count and check recently posted content.

14. Schedule Posts in Advance

One of the most efficient ways to run a Facebook business page is to schedule your posts in advance either weekly or monthly. There are lots of last minute things which come upand can distract us away from a fixed schedule. This may pose a challenge to the pursuit of posting a steady stream of relevant and interesting content designed to engage your target audience.

Once you've identified the best time to post on Facebook, use applications such as HubSpot, Buffer or Hootsuite to schedule your posts for a particular date and time weekly or monthly. You can create an editorial calendar for the entire month. Consider festivals, holidays, and events etc. for the month while planning "hot" or viral posts in advance. The posts can be planned at the same time in advance every week for the entire week.

However, having said that, maintain a balance between pre-scheduled and timely posts to avoid turning your page into an automated machine where it loses a human touch. Ensure you're creating some real time posts too for engaging with fans or striking up a conversation to get their views on a recent development.

How to schedule posts in advance?

Start creating a post as you normally would.

Click on the down arrow sign located adjacent to Publish, and tap on Schedule.

Just below publication, choose the date and time when you wish to publish the post.

Select Schedule

You can also delete or make changes to scheduled posts.

Click edit to make changes to your post or select the down arrow icon to reschedule or delete the post.

Chapter Three:

13 Fantastic Tips for Boosting Engagement

It is little wonder that Facebook is among the most dominant content marketing platforms. The social networking site has a ton of fresh, dynamic and resourceful features that can be brilliantly integrated into your overall promotional strategy. Yes, we all know by now that it can be used to increase engagement, boost authority and build brands. Your half a million fans will be of little consequence if they aren't doing much on the page.

Have you ever thought about why some posts go viral, while others become ghost towns? Nope, it has got little to do with luck, and more to do with the timing of your post, the words you use and what is posted.

Facebook users react well to posts related to technology, travel/lifestyle, health, positivity and sports/games. A quick pro tip – if you include words such as "why", "how" or "most" on your posts, you are likely to garner higher likes, comments, and shares.

The million-dollar question is – how can you boost engagement through Facebook posts?

Here are 12 fantastic and proven tips to help boost your audience engagement.

1. Host Contests

This is one of the best strategies for improving engagement on your Facebook business page. It's such a no-brainer, yet marketers fail to channelize it effectively. The thrill of winning something gets people to take action, which can be used to your advantage. Use rewards, prizes, and freebies as an incentive to create a buzz about your brand.

One of the biggest advantages for marketers is that for a comparatively low-cost, you'll end up gaining plenty of exposure and brand awareness. If done right, it can be a brilliant payoff.

How to Create a Facebook Contest

1. Pick the Right Prize

The prize is what's going to make or ensure a successful run for your contest. Keep it relevant and appropriate to your business. A pro tip is to offer your audience gift cards for your business, which gives them a chance to get interested in or try your products/services.

Offering customers free iPads and iPhones will have them liking iPads and iPhones, not really your products or services. They may simply like your page or share your post for the sake of winning an iPhone without really being interested in your products or services.

However, if you are offering gift cards or freebies related to your products or services, you will get a bunch of targeted, interested customers who are interested in trying your products. For instance, if you sell baby care products and offer gift vouchers for the same, you'll get a ton of interested parents who are keen on trying your products liking your page or sharing your posts.

Giving prizes that are not relevant to your products or services won't really help boost conversions. However, a bunch of targeted consumers trying your products can help spread the word about them, especially in the initial stages of the business. You can include discounts or freebies on future purchases in the gift card too for encouraging customers to buy from you.

2. Make it Easy to Enter

Your aim is to increase the number of followers/fans and boost engagement for your business page. Make entering the contest easy for people to gain maximum response. You can ask social media users to like your page, share the contest post and tag friends who you think will be interested in the contest to be eligible for the contest/draw. Pick a winner by conducting a live draw.

Another popular way to get people to participate in contests is by focusing on user generated content. This is also a smart strategy for populating your business page with interesting content posted by users themselves. Ask customers to enter the draw by posting images, videos or slogans to enter. Create a hashtag, and let views use the hashtag while posting content on your business page. The audience can then vote for their favorite entry.

Include brief information about how to enter the contest on your post, and link to an outside web page for details about rules and regulations to avoid cluttering the Facebook contest post.

3. Attention Grabbing Title

A short, catchy call-to-action title helps maximize your contest response. For instance, "Enter to Win a $60 Gift Card For Our Fabulous Range of Handmade Soaps." It's simple, descriptive and appealing. It tells visitors what they are supposed to do and the prize that awaits them in a straightforward manner.

You can also create a contest entry landing page, and ask them to enter their contact details. This will help you create an email list of people who may be interested in learning more about your products or services in future. Send people on email list updates, seasonal offers, and informative newsletters to keep them hooked.

4. Image

Use large, high-quality images to entice people into entering the contest. If you are giving away gift cards, use a large image of the gift card with its worth mentioned prominently on the image. Also, include images of products that were purchased for the given gift card amount.

2. Post Response Generating Posts

Pose an attention-grabbing yet simple question for drawing your fans into a conversation. For instance, if you run a travel/lifestyle/leisure related brand, posting images related to beaches or mountains with a simple caption like, "Hit Like if you want to spend a relaxed day on this tropical island" or "Hit like if you feel like grabbing an ice-cream Sundae Right Now." Simple yes/no type of questions can also help generate quick Facebook post traction.

Telling people what you want them to do will increase your page engagement. Ask interesting open questions, such as, "If you could take off to any destination of your choice, where would it be? Or "What food items are on your current craving list?" Keep posts engaging and relevant to your page.

Which is your favorite luxury car?

You can never really have enough ---------

How many times do you let the phone ring before answering?

Questions like these spark stimulating conversations and unimaginably funny answers. Get creative with your questions to draw your fans into a conversation.

Create posts that get people involved. If you are stuck with a decision, create a poll to gather feedback from your target audience. It gives you quick insights about exactly what your customers are looking for, along with boosting page engagement. Encourage fans to post testimonials of your products or services along with images.

If there's a raging topical issue or controversy related to your field, ask customers to share their views about the same. Keep the debate sane and healthy by establishing clear guidelines at the outset.

Urge people to share memories, moments and experiences or go slightly edgy with a controversial question. Ask direct questions or encourage people to share their favorite tips related to your products/services.

Make people feel wonderful about them by encouraging them to share innovative ideas about the different ways through which they use your products. You bet people love it when the spotlight's on them or when they are at the center of the conversation.

I simply love asking my page fans to pick between two choices. Pick a favorite between "A" or "B" or choose between "X" or "Y." This can create a lovely division between fans (evil in a fun way yes), which sparks further debate and conversation in the comments. Using current controversies is alright as long as you don't venture into sensitive topics such as politics and religion.

Whether your post bags a single comment or multiple comments, attempt to respond to each of them individually. Facebook lets you like comments, which is a great way for you to acknowledge their response. Of course, it will be a challenge to reply to hundreds of comments. However, taking that extra effort will make you come across as a caring, customer-focused organization that values its fans/buyers.

3. Post Shareable Content

Videos and infographics are currently the hottest content formats on the social media. If you can create a single infographic or list for summarizing everything that people need to know about a topic, there's no stopping fans from sharing it. Checklists or cheat-sheets are amazing from a viral perspective.

If your business relates to travel gear, you can create a handy backpacker's checklist or if you are an internet marketer, a quick content creation or topic generation (or headline generation) cheat sheet can do the trick.

Make it a valuable proposition for your target audience by putting together information that is time-consuming to research in an easily digestible format. For instance, you can put together a handy guide for travelers visiting a particular destination by including all important information in a single infographic.

People don't have the time to research and jot down important pieces of information on a single source, which is why infographics are hugely popular. You can create an infographic using an app like Canva or hire someone to do it.

4. Engage with Other Businesses

There's no stopping you from engaging on other pages, especially when they there's a synergy of products/services or a shared audience. For instance, if a wedding jewelry related business has posted something about weddings, you can chime in with your 2 cents too if you are a florist, wedding photographer or wedding cakes business. You aren't directly competing with the brand or there's no conflict of interest.

However, be mindful of not spamming other business pages on the Facebook landscape with your promotional posts. Keep it subtle and engage in a naturally meaningful manner. Add well-researched, detailed and thought-provoking comments to establish authority. You'll expose your brand to a large number of targeted customers if it's a popular page.

Who doesn't benefit from a bit of cross promotion and synergy? Encourage other pages within your industry to comment/post on your pages too. If you can work out a fruitful mutual sharing agreement, both pages can boost their organic reach and enjoy exposure to a wider base of potential customers. You can also create guest posts for other blogs, which they can share on their business page to increase your authority, credibility and brand awareness.

Round-ups are another fantastic way to get experts to share your posts on their pages. Ask influencers in your field to share their best tips on the given topic. Make a post about these tips by tagging these influencers and getting them to share the round-up on their pages.

Everyone loves to be seen as an expert among their fans and audience, which means the influencers will most likely share these posts (which pitch them as an expert) on their news feed, thus giving your brand exposure among fans/followers of a bunch of experts or popular business pages.

If you find particularly interesting images on your fan's news feed, take permission to post it and give them credit for it. Social media is based on a strong sharing economy, which means you mustn't shy away from posting relevant, valuable and useful content from other players in the niche.

One pro tip to get a lot of organic likes for your page is to enable the "Similar Page Suggestions" on your page. Go to "Settings" and enable the "Similar Page Suggestions" option. This way when people like pages that are similar to yours, Facebook automatically suggests your page to them. Not many people know about this feature but it can help you some great organic likes from interested folks.

5. Boost Posts

Facebook offers business page administrators/owners a paid boost post option to create more engagement on specific posts. You can either boost posts among existing followers and their friends (which means the post will be visible to a higher number of fans on their feed) or select a predefined audience (based on audience demographics, interests, hobbies, and pages they've liked) to boost your posts. These posts will show up on the news feed on the selected audience group, which means a higher engagement for your posts.

Boost your most popular blog posts that have witnessed a considerable swarm of traffic. Post it on your business page, and use the boost post option. There's no need to invest thousands of dollars on advertising. You can start with $25 by targeting folks who've already liked your page and people on their friends list. It may be enough to give your posts a slight nudge.

Though there's low chance of seeing thousands of likes or share, boosting posts can increase engagement and initiate conversation. It can get people to spark a conversation, while also making them aware of your products or services. This can increase your organic reach within their networks. Use this strategy for high-quality, information blogs where you are offering clear solutions to desperate problems faced by people. It works well for posts that answer the most compelling questions about a topic or offer people high-value takeaways.

How do you look for your blog's most popular content? Go to Google Analytics. Select Behavior, followed by Site Content and All Pages. Go through the metrics for every page to know your most popular posts.

How to boost posts on Facebook? Here's a handy step by guide to get you started.

Go to your business page

Select the post you wish to boost (remember to pick only high-quality posts which have proved their popularity on your web page or posts you think have the potential to be popular).

Select the "Boost Post" button located just above the post. If the button isn't activated, it will stay unclickable, which simply means that this particular post cannot be boosted. There can be several reasons for this including the like the business page may be unpublished or you may not have sufficient admin rights to boost a post or you may need to set up a payout method.

Go to the Audience field. Carefully pick the audience you would like to reach from the given options. There's also an option to "Create New Audience." You can start from scratch by targeting users based on their location age, interests, gender and behavior.

Next, click the dropdown to pick a budget for boosting your post. You can either select a predefined budget or opt for the "Choose Your Own" optionand enter an amount of your choice.

Pick a duration for which you want the post to be boosted. Enter the end date of the boosted post in the "Run this ad until" section.

Select a preferred payment method from the given options. If you haven't done any paid promotions on Facebook before, you'll have to add a payment method to your Facebook ads account.

Finally, click "Boost."

6. Stay Persistent

You won't believe how many people actually give up building strong business pages on Facebook when they would've been a roaring success simply by tweaking their strategy a bit. Don't expect overnight success. It's not like you build a page, and have people swarming to it with a million likes and thousands of shares. Many of your initial posts will barely have any engagement. Keep posting a variety of stuff to test what works best for your market.

If a particular type of post hasn't performed well, opt for another. See what other businesses in your domain are doing successfully and incorporate the same into your social media content strategy.

While social media marketers will also emphasize on posting relevant posts (including yours truly), it's alright to have fun occasionally. Experiment with a funny quote or laugh-worthy meme that your fans can relate to. Pose random questions.

Don't always keep the focus on your products or services. Help you fans have some fun! You may not get business through that funny meme but it makes you likable. It will set the tone for another post, which can include a link to your website.

People generally use Facebook to make connections and browse through informative and entertaining posts. Try different types of posts to measure ones that draw a maximum response from your target audience or stir them into interaction.

Facebook offers some of the best audience insights and analytics for your page. Spot patterns and trends, and reinvent for strategy according to these valuable insights. For example, if you see a huge surge in fans within the week, look closely at your recently posted content. Figure out a clear reason for these trends, and continue posting more of the same if it's working.

Where do I check my Facebook business page insights?

Log in to your Facebook account.

Click the page for which you want to view the statistics from the left sidebar.

Click "View Insights" on the right sidebar of your business page to check interaction statistics for the last month. The statistics will include insights such as number of new likes, post views and other user activity represented through figures and charts.

Social media is all about creating a run-up to the actual decision. You're setting the stage by establishing relationships, engaging your audience and making your brand desirable before you actually go for the kill. Remember the 80-20 rule?

10. Post at the Optimal Time

Posting at a time when your audience is most likely to be on Facebook increases the visibility and exposure of your message. This is a question most newbie marketers struggle with simply because there isn't a single time for all enterprises. The best days and times to post on Facebook depends on the type of business.

For instance, if you are targeting home-makers, they are likely to be online at a different time (later mornings or afternoons) than working professionals (late evenings and weekends). It also depends on the type of post you are targeting, and the region the post is meant for.

There is, of course, some reliable data on the best times to post on Facebook, though you must research the social media browsing habits of your target audience to arrive at the best days and times unique to your business.

As a general guideline, the optimal time to post content on Facebook is 3.00 p.m. on Wednesdays. Other good days and times to post are 12:00 to 1:00 p.m. on weekends, and 1:00 to 4:00 p.m. on Fridays and Thursdays.

Engagement rates are known to be 18% higher towards the fag-end of the week (Thursday and Friday), and on other weekdays from 1:00 to 4:00 p.m. This is especially true for businesses related to leisure, travel, vacations, and hobbies. The click through rates are known to be higher at the above mentioned times. Also, since there is 10% increase in Facebook activity on Fridays (and people tend to be merrier at the prospect of the oncoming weekend), it is generally considered a good day for posting positive, funny and uplifting content.

The most unfavorable times to post on Facebook include after 8:00 p.m. and after 8:00 a.m. on weekends. Of course, use this as a general guideline and not rule of the book for posting on your business page.

You still need to investigate what are the best times for audience engagement based on trial and error. Try posting at different times during the first few days, and check when you can elicit the maximum response or engagement from your target audience.

If you are beginning from scratch and have no data of your own to gauge what the audience likes or dislikes, simply go to a platform like BuzzSumo.com. Do a search based on your niche or main keywords, and find a list of posts which have received maximum likes and shares on Facebook.

The platform offers tons of features, including the check which pages/posts are performing particularly well for a competitor.

It is also a nice place to find influencers in your domain for some much-needed cross promotions.

11. Keep Posts Short

Don't convert your Facebook business page into a blog. Social media users are not on Facebook to read long-winded content. Keep it concise and engaging. Posts that are under 50 characters garner maximum engagement. Adding characters beyond that reduces your chances of engagement. Unless long posts have proven to work for your particular niche or audience, it is best to keep them below 50 characters.

Don't sound preachy or overly promotional; inspire people to connect with you by sharing stories visually.

Share images based on the core values related to your business. You'll be the ultimate social media magnet if you share the business/brand's passion with customers, creating an almost cult like following. Your business can be passionate about organic food (if you run a food related business). Build a community by infusing the same level of passion in your followers through short and interesting posts.

Share a sense of purpose that genuinely inspires people. In the above example, it can be about healthy eating, going organic or sticking to vegan meals. Find a clear sense of purpose and spread it to your fans. Post pictures of your brand connecting with real people to add the much-needed human touch. Share uplifting and inspiring quotes that trigger your fans into action.

List posts, infographics and "how to" articles that stir curiosity fare effectively on the Facebook platform. If you do a BuzzSumo search for "healthy eating", you'll discover that the top-performing posts are "18 Make Ahead Meals to Eat Healthy without Even Trying" and "How to Eat Healthy Whole Foods, Plant-Based Diet on $50 Per Week?" Well, everyone wants to know how one can eat healthy on a budget of $50/week. Spark a sense of curiosity, and you'll have them hooked.

12. Use the Power of Facebook Groups

Groups are an excellent platform for building a community based on shared interests. They bring together people sharing a common passion and can stir greater dialogue and engagement than regular business pages. Track down niche groups related to your industry or create your own group, and link it to your main business page.

Give it an easily searchable and relevant name. Include a brief and appropriate description for the group so people can find it easily. Keep posting content that inspires interaction about topics related to the group. Encourage group members to post their queries or start a discussion. You can even share your blog posts or business page posts within the group to give them greater exposure.

Building a loyal and engaged community is the foundation of launching a successful social media enterprise. Though maintaining a busy group can be time-consuming and tedious, it may offer brilliant pay offs in future.

Groups are incredible when it comes to building a network around your business. For instance, if you are a consultant for small and mid-sized businesses, you can build a group around "power entrepreneurs." Similarly, if you sell camping gear or organize camping holidays, start a "camping enthusiasts" group. Encourage people to share their blogs, inspiring pieces of content and topics that get everyone fired up into a discussion.

How to get the group rolling?

- Post questions. If you don't know what to talk about, simply ask people what they'd like to discuss.

- Host events such as an online webinar, Hangout session or in person events. Groups give you a fabulous opportunity to connect with like-minded folks in person.

- Encourage member introductions. Ask people to share a little bit of their background, passions and business interests. Create conversations and/or connections based on sharing details about people's aspirations, goals, and interests.

- Conduct polls about what people would like to hear about and discuss in the group.

13. Celebrate Holidays and Festivals

Fans love it when you add a bit of holiday/festival cheer to your posts. It gets them into a joyful and celebratory mode. Ensure to create posts for special events, and participate in the festive spirit. It reveals an interesting persona, while also demonstrating your sense of awareness about the latest happenings. This makes the business look more human and less robotic, which is really what social media marketing is about.

Find out if the holiday applies to a particular community or it's celebrated globally. Use it as an occasion to greet you fans and connect with them.

For instance, if it's International Women's Day, you can share an appreciation post about the company's women employees. Give a brief and interesting backdrop, and mention how they add value to the organization. Fans love inside details about people who run the show from behind the scenes.

People are generally in a more joyous, positive and spending mode during festivals, which means it may be easier to get them to make purchases in a promotional post, following a cheery festival wish post.

Chapter Four:

Killing it with Facebook Advertising

It is no secret that Facebook offers one of the best paid advertising programs on the internet. The biggest advantage of opting for a paid promotion is that you can target your customers based on just about anything on their profile from the kind of movies they enjoy watching to life events (recently married or engaged) to their profession and interests. Wait, there's more – think birthdays, zip code, relationship status, and education.

This gives marketers looking to target a specific group a clear edge for promoting their products and services. Facebook is a goldmine for smart marketers who know how to use its comprehensive user database to their advantage.

Take for example, you own a gymnasium in Phoenix, and want to target health buffs that have moved to the city recently, you can target your ads only towards them. Similarly, if you sell golf kits online throughout the United States, you can target golf enthusiasts living in the country.

This saves you from throwing away precious advertising money by promoting your products/services to people who have scant interest in them. There's no denying that Facebook's ads can be super profitable if you know how to play with them effectively.

According to an eMarket survey, almost 96% of social media users consider Facebook advertising as the most result-generating paid promotion methods across multiple social media platforms.

A *New York Times* report states that on an average, users typically spend an hour on Facebook each day, which explains why Facebook advertising budgets are skyrocketing. You are leaving too much money on the table for competitors if you aren't leveraging the power of Facebook advertising.

You know why people hate YouTube ads? Because they interrupt a user's viewing experience. Facebook has tweaked their advertising feature to seamlessly and naturally integrate its paid promotions into a user's news feed without disrupting his experience. This is why viewers are less annoyed and more receptive to these ads.

So, what are the best tips to get started with Facebook advertising? I've got your back here too.

Here's a handy guide to help you advertise like a pro on Facebook.

1. To begin advertising on Facebook, go to your page's "Ads Manager" section.

2. Before you begin advertising, you must have a clear objective for the paid promotion.

What do you hope to achieve through the paid promotion? More page likes? More engagement on specific posts? Higher website conversions? App installations and other similar marketing goals.

Once you pick your advertising goal, Facebook will display the option that works best for accomplishing your marketing objective.

3. Pick your audience. In the beginning, you'll have to test various audience groups to identify the ones which produce optimal results. Based on the criteria specified by you, Facebook will present an Audience Definition tool to the right of the audience field option. It takes all you pre-defined properties to come up with a potential reach figure.

Facebook's audience targeting fields are so vast, it's virtually impossible to include them all here. You can target users based on their location, gender, languages, relationships, finances, ethnicity, life events, politics, interests, hobbies, connections, behavior and much more.

There is a Custom Audience option too where you target a set of predefined audience members in your organization's database or people who've visited your blog or used your application. This option allows you to target customers based on very specific criteria.

Once you've discovered an audience group that has responded well to your ads, you can save these audiences by clicking on saving the audience group for later (so you don't have to go through the process of picking the audience all over again).

Pro tip – While the campaign is running, if you gauge that a particular group is responding really well to the ad and bringing down your cost per like/click, you can edit your audience options instantly. For instance, say you are promoting an adventure travel page and learn that men are offering a lower cost per click for your page. You may want to edit your audience settings to men only.

4. Facebook offers you the option to select how and where you want your ads to appear. Advertisers have the option of picking desktop feed, mobile feed, and right column ads.

You can select the ones that are most beneficial for your business, but mobile feed ads perform much better than desktop feed ads or right column ads (least favorable). Most people access their social media accounts through handheld devices, which makes mobile feed ads effective.

5. Set a daily budget. If you want your ad to run on a daily budget, specify your daily limit in the Daily Budget option. For instance, if you enter $25 as your daily budget, Facebook will run an ad on a daily budget of $25 until you end the campaign.

If you want the campaign to run for a fixed number of days, enter the end date within the "Run Campaign Until" option. Your ad will only run until a specified date. When you're experimenting in the beginning, go with a modest budget.

6. Creating the ad. NNo rocket science this. Your headline has to be enticing enough to compel users to take their eyes off other interesting stuff on their news feed. The best trick is to tap into the underlying primary motives of your target audience. What is it that stirs your audience emotionally, logically and physically? What makes them sit up, take notice and act? Well yes, the most common and effective primal emotions are lust, greed, fear, sorrow, guilt, and happiness. Channelize these emotions, while also presenting a logical solution. Offer immediate gratification to grab their attention.

How to Create A Blockbuster WordPress Blog in Under 20 Minutes.

Save $12000 Daily on Facebook Fans by Avoiding This Costly Mistake.

Pose question-based headlines while promising to offer a solution.

Tired of Living in Debt? Like Us to Know How to Live a Debt-Free Life!

Do you know the number one emotion that drives people to make purchase related decisions? Fear it is.

Yes, fear is an extremely powerful emotion when it comes to getting people to act upon something. People aren't too open to the prospect of investing in new products because they fear losing money or to make a wrong decision. This is exactly the psychology behind why free products are such a rage when it comes to grabbing the prospective customer's attention.

Free means zero risk, and no risk means zero fear. Headlines offering freebies or free solutions to the user's problems perform brilliantly because there's no risk attached to it.

Keep the copy tight, succinct and engaging (photo ads have a limit of 90 characters). Use clear, straightforward language that's easy to understand. It should trigger your audience's, while also telling them the benefits they can enjoy by liking your or visiting your website. Follow the powerful WIFM (What's In It For Me) principle. Keep it brief with a high lead value.

Facebook has also come up with slideshow ads, where you can create a PowerPoint style slideshow with your best images.

Active wear brand Carbon 38 discovered that in comparison to the regular photo ads, slideshow ads offer an 85 percent higher return on your ad spend and a 40 percent increase in click-through rate.

A lot of business and Facebook ventures are converting their most popular content pieces into slideshow ads. You are simply distilling and repackaging your best content into an ad. Think of creative ways to convey the written message into visuals or sum up each point in a few words, and make a killer video ad out of it. Keep the content throughout the video consistent with the final call to action.

Click on the preview option at the bottom of the ad to ensure everything looks good. If you're happy with how the ad looks, tap the "Confirm" button to submit the ad. When the ad is approved by Facebook, you get a notification for the same.

7. Split test multiple ads. Split testing or A/B testing as it's referred to is testing two different ads to conclude which one performs better. It virtually impossible to predict what works and what doesn't even if you know your audience really well. The only way to create profitable ad campaigns is by testing different options to pick out ones that work. You'll know which ads work and which don't when you try various options through split testing.

to make the most of Facebook's split test feature, create different variations of ads that are performing well by altering a single attribute at one time. For instance, pick an ad that's performing well, and create two versions of it by retaining everything else but using two different headlines for both versions.

If you make too many changes in both versions, you won't be able to single out elements that are working well. In the above example, if you were to alter the headline and ad copy, and one ad performs clearly well over the other, you won't know if it was due to the headline or ad copy. Stick to testing a single element at one time.

You can also split test various ad placement options. Have one campaign running for right column ads, another for mobile news feed ads and still another for desktop news feed ads. This strategy allows you to closely monitor your budget than if all options are merged into a single campaign.

8. Use the psychology of visuals and colors to your benefit. Facebook ad pros will share little about the brilliant psychological persuasion powers of specific colors (these are their insider secrets you see). However, I am about to reveal one of the most powerful creative elements of Facebook advertising that almost every successful advertiser is harnessing. The power of visuals and colors. Did you know that 90% of all quick judgments we make related to products/brands are traced back to the most dominant colors in the ad or business logo?

According to a study published in Management Decision, there are some clear scientifically backed trends related to how colors are perceived by different people. While the younger audience prefers bright, flaming shades such as red, orange, and yellow, older folks like cooler colors like green, blue, and purple. With age, people tend to prefer cooler, darker shades.

If you are a fun, peppy youth centric brand, you may want to include bright shades in your Facebook ad. However, keep in mind that just because blue signifies trust, reliability, and dependability, you can't use it if it doesn't fit well with the products you are marketing.

For instance, food product logos and pictures almost always feature bright, flaming colors (red, orange, yellow) that are said to stimulate hunger. Blue is not said to get well with food products as it's associated with poison and chemicals. Find colors that fit your brand's personality, and use them in your ad design, images, and logo. It all boils down to the appropriateness and personal fit. Think about your target audience and use colors that evoke the right psychological triggers in them to expedite their buying decisions.

Chapter Five:

4 Clever Ways to Make Money On Facebook

You know by now that though Facebook is great for sharing pictures of your vacation or establishing connections with old friends, there's a lot of money to be made here by building brands and businesses.

Here are some 10 ingenious ways to turn Facebook into a profit machine.

1. Sell Other People's Products and Services

You've probably heard of affiliate marketing if you have been following the world of internet marketing for a while. It is a fairly profitable business model, where you get a commission for selling other people's products or services.

There are plenty of affiliate marketing marketplaces (such as ClickBank, ShareASale, MaxBounty etc) where you can sign up to promote a variety of products and services. You can also sign up as an affiliate for programs directly through their site if they accept affiliates.

Here are some general guidelines for picking affiliate marketing products on Clickbank

Pick products that have a commission percentage of 50 percent and above except if it's a recurring commission based service/product (in which case you can bring it down to 40 percent). Anything lower than 50-60 percent that is just not worth the time.

Opt for a product with high gravity ratings. These are the products that are performing really well and making affiliate marketers money. However, don't strike off new products with low gravity ratings from your list. They may have a high potential and little competition.

It all boils down to the quality of the sales page and product. If you find a product promising and beneficial for your audience, experiment with it.

When you sign up to be an affiliate or promoter for any product/service, the merchant or marketplace site gives you a unique affiliate link (through which your sales and other stats can be monitored). You include this link in your blog or Facebook posts along with interesting, valuable content. Each time someone makes a purchase by clicking on your unique link, you earn a commission.

Once you've picked your products, build a fan page or community on a topic related to the products/services. For instance, if you are selling a course for copywriters, you may want to create a page or group for copywriting enthusiasts or beginners.

You can offer lots of copywriting tips, content creation ideas etc to win their trust and build authority. Once you've engaged your audience, positioned yourself as an authority and won their trust, it's easy to recommend things to them.

Create a detailed review for the post, and share a link on your fan page or group. Include an impact headline that sums up how the course can help copywriters get started in a profitable industry.

Facebook allows you to share affiliate links as of now as long as it complies with their community standards. Read through their policies first before promoting products and services through affiliate marketing.

There are tons of fan pages dedicated to cars, drones, relationships, homes and just about any topic under the sun. Find a bunch of passionate fans who have a deep interest in the topic, build a strong community around it to gain trust and loyalty, and finally, start promoting high-quality products/services which you think will benefit your audience.

Create a blog around the topic and instead of sending people straight to the buyer page, drive them to your blog post where they can get in-depth information about a topic. The affiliate marketing link can be placed on the blog or at the end of it.

No one like to see tacky looking, long winded links on a Facebook page. Make your links short and professional looking by using a link cloaker software to dress up tawdry affiliate links.

If you are selling more than a single product or service, create separate pages for each program or category of programs. For instance, if you are selling digital products or eBooks related to toddler parenting, create fan page or group for parents of toddlers.

Similarly, cooking related products/services can be combined into a separate group for cooking enthusiasts. This way you are sub-targeting various niches. People don't want to like your page to see a bunch of promotions that they aren't interested in.

You can, of course, repost and share things that are common to groups. For instance, if you come with a post such, "10 Healthy Recipes that Will Get Your toddlers to Lick Their Fingers", it can fit in the cooking as well as parenting page. Do you get the flow?

One of the most important things to keep in mind if you are using affiliate marketing to make money on Facebook is to understand that it is your reputation at stake as an influencer and brand, which means stick to selling only high-quality and valuable products that truly benefit your audience. Don't end up peddling a load of bull or you'll lose these precious audience members and your reputation.

2. Write and Sell eBooks

eBooks are becoming insanely profitable off late owing to the low upfront operational costs involved. There's no cost related to printing and materials since everything is shared electronically. This means anyone with a decent topic or idea can attempt to create an ebook. Plus, it's a nice passive income stream, where you invest some effort to create the book once but reap its benefits forever or each time it's sold.

with its targeted audience and community feel, Facebook has a ready audience for your books if you know how to penetrate the market.

Nonfiction eBooks that offer people how to information or a clear solution to their pressing woes tend to sell well. Currently, the best selling eBooks are books that tell people how to make money with eBooks, which means everyone is interested in savoring a slice of the profitable eBook pie. Unless you have a really gripping tale, a knack for building strong characters, stick to nonfiction.

Start by writing your eBook on a topic or area where you already have some established authority. You don't need shiny credentials to be an eBook author but you should be able to convince people about why they should buy from you over any regular Joe who also writes books. Positioning yourself as an expert will give you an edge when it comes to promoting the book.

Once you've finished drafting your book in a word processor, create a Kindle Direct Publishing account and add your book by following the instructions under Bookshelf < Add New Title.

KDP allows publishers to earn a royalty of 70% if the eBook is priced below $9.99. Keep the price low initially to bag some early bird reviews and ratings, and notch it up once the book gains some traction.

Now comes the fun part. Promoting your book on Facebook. Like all businesses, start by building a community around the topic of your eBook. If it's about flying drones, build a community of people who are passionate about drones.

Here are some smart strategies to promote your eBook on Facebook

Giveaways

No surprise this, people love freebies and giveaways. Distribute a few free copies on the book to loyal and dedicated fans on your page, along with influencers in the niche. Request them to leave behind reviews, and ratings. Kindle Publishing has its own unique algorithms, where if a particular book performs well, Amazon gives it further push by recommending it to customers. If sales soar, it becomes a part of the best selling list.

Consider building an email list through Facebook, where you can communicate with interested readers about updates, news, promotional offers, new launches and informative newsletters.

Also, host sweepstakes and giveaways contests for a copy of the book or other freebies related to the book. Ensure every promotional post has a clear Call to Action, where your audience know exactly what they are supposed to do. Include a mind-blowing eBook cover. Promote the giveaway extensively on your newsletter, blog and social media. Always tag winners in the comments, while also sending them a personal message.

Contests are a great way to get people excited about being a part of your email list. For instance, a pet based business can ask pet owners to send entries for the cutest cat or dog contest. All the photographs can be posted on your Facebook page, and winners can be picked by asking your followers to vote for their favorite picture.

Tabs

Create a separate Tab on your fan page for the book. Let your readers know you as an author and learn more the book. The additional tabs show up right under your Facebook cover image, and can be expanded to offer additional information once users click "More." Visitors can browse through the entire page and explore content that's useful to them. Use this tab feature to your advantage for promoting the book.

Keep your Facebook posts brief and gripping, and add detailed information under specifically created tabs. This way people who want additional information about your products and services can click on relevant tabs for details. Tabs help keep your information distinct and organized. You don't need to cram everything on a single page. Just create a separate tab for each of your books, and make it easy for people to find more information.

Facebook Videos

Apart from using advertising strategies mentioned in the previous chapter to promote your eBooks, readers can also use videos brilliantly to create a buzz about their books. It is such an interesting way to create curiosity about your book, yet marketers fail to cash in on it. Play with 15-second video ads or create interesting video content that piques your audience's curiosity about the book. Don't forget to use the autoplay feature while creating video ads.

You can talk about the highlights of the book in the video. Talk to your customers in an interest grabbing and conversational manner about how they benefit from the book. Introduce a sense of urgency in your voice and tone towards the end of the video when you urge them to take action right away. These videos may give you a better response or conversion rate than direct sales or blatantly promotional runs.

Create Bundle Offers

Creating offers is another cool trick to stay on top of the Facebook eBook marketing/promotional game. You may have more than one book in your eBook portfolio, which means you can bundle them up with smart promotional strategies.

For instance, if customers purchase your first book within the stipulated period, you can offer the next two books for 50 percent off the regular price tag. This will increase the sales of all three books. You can also offer a free copy of the next book.

Offers create a nice buzz for your book on Facebookand help spread a positive word about it. Here's an example – Claim your free copy of my latest book today!

Send the customer to a landing page, where he can claim a copy of your next book by purchasing a copy of your current book.

Focused Groups

Groups offer a precise, targeted and dedicated platform for promoting your eBook. There are literally hundreds of groups/communities on Facebook dedicated to independent authors/publishers, multiple genres, and even well-known authors. Be active in these groups where you can come across several beneficial cross-promotional activities.

It's also a good practice to comment on these groups, engage in group discussions and basically strike a rapport with your target readers.

Keep in mind a few points though before using groups to promote and market your books. First, is your book relevant to the audience of that particular group? If you've created an eBook about taking a luxury cruise holiday, you certainly won't find your audience in a backpacker's group or adventure vacation enthusiasts group.

Find the relevant groups, and increase your conversions by introducing your book to the right audience.

Next, some groups do not take too kindly to overtly promotional posts or promotional links. Always take the time to learn about the group's etiquette and rules before posting or you risk getting banned from the group, thus resulting in an unfavorable reputation. Create your own fan page as an author once you gain considerable popularity.

3. Build an Email List

Building an email list is one of the best ways to establish constant communication with your customers. You can make money by selling physical or digital products on your blog or promote other people's products/services or make money through advertising programs such as Google Adsense if you have a targeted email list of people who are interested in your products or services.

Offer a lead magnet such as a freebie, coupon, eBook, special report etc. much like any opt-in form to entice customers to be a part of your power list. Make it something that's hard to find. Some internet marketing blogs offer their customers a list of the hottest niches for blogs, while others offer free themes, plugins etc. It really depends on exactly what your target audience is after. Give them rare, well-researched and valuable tools, and they'll bite the hook.

Offering exclusive and hard to find content (remember the list of the best performing niches?) in a downloadable format is a great way to offer customers solid value, and get them to return the favor by buying from your or visiting your blog. Not all business deal with physical products, which makes giving away exclusive pieces of content highly lucrative.

Another smart trick you can use is adding a link to your squeeze or lead capture page. Edit your cover image by adding a relevant description for the photo. Include a powerful call to action within the description, followed by a squeeze page link. This will not just give you instant branding on the cover photograph, but also help people reach your opt-in page easily.

You can also include a call to across on your cover photo instead of including it in the description. This way it's prominently displayed across the top of your page as soon as people visit your page, which creates a sense of urgency. You're basically goading people to act fast by including a clear and conspicuous call to action.

Facebook can also be used to retain and build connections with people on your list. When people opt in to your list, send them a welcome email that prompts them to follow you on Facebook and other social media platforms. One of the biggest advantages of this neat tip is even if they unsubscribe from your list in future, they will still receive updates on Facebook and other social media platforms.

Whet your audience's appetite by showing them exactly what they'll get if they sign up for your email list. Share your newsletter on Facebook. The caption should include a link to your opt-in page. What's more? Your Facebook fans will share your newsletter and give you, even more, exposure and subscribers from among their social contacts.

If you are offering a piece of content that's not available anywhere in your upcoming newsletter, use that as bait for signing up people for your email list. This strategy serves a dual purpose. It piques the curiosity of people who aren't on your email list and subsequently gets them to sign up for the list.

Additionally, people who are on your list and haven't been too responsive will also get curious owing to the buzz. They will end up opening a newsletter they wouldn't have bothered about otherwise.

Host Events

Hosting events like an online webinar or creating a real, physical event on Facebook is also a great way of connecting with your target audience, and getting their details. Several internet marketers successfully advertise free webinars using Facebook's advertising feature. Encourage fans to sign up for a free training or webinar by entering their email.

A free webinar can be advertised like –

Free Training Webinar

Has your online business hit a slump? Looking to shake things up a bit? Instagram could just be what you need to go from average to stupendous.

Join Instagram marketing expert (name) for a stellar, value-packed FREE webinar this Friday at 7:00 pm PST where you can learn some of the fastest ways to skyrocket your business with Instagram. See you there.

Create a post promoting a free webinar and boost the post or send your visitors to a lead opt-in form through Facebook ads.

Why tap online resources? You can also create Facebook events for networking in your city or neighborhood. While registering online for the event, people can be encouraged to opt in to your email list.

4. Sell Physical Products on Facebook

Facebook isn't only about content and connections, there's a whole new market out there for physical products too.

You can create an attractive, comprehensive and targeted virtual storefront on Facebook using an ecommerce platform like Shopify. Many of these ecommerce platforms offer you a free trial to gauge how

The best part about setting up a Facebook store is you can reach a global audience, while constantly engaging with them and growing your business.

How to Create a Facebook Store or Shop Page?

First, log in to your business page. On the timeline just below your page cover photo, there's a section called "Add Shop Section."

Click the blue "Add Shop Section" on the pop-up.

Enter all the required business details.

You need to set-up a payment system next.

The only available payment option on Facebook currently is Stripe, which means you will have to register for a Stripe account if you don't have one already. Set up the payment system.

Once the Stripe account has been set-up, Facebook will redirect you to the main business page. Click on Finish Setup to fill in the remaining details.

You're all set to start selling now!

You should now see a separate "Shop" tab on your business page. Click on the tab and you'll get a box that asks you to add a product to the shop. Click on the "Add Product" link to continue.

Once you click "Add Photos", you can start uploading product images. After uploading images, click on "Use Photos" for your images to go live.

You'll get a "Product Details" field once you've uploaded all images. Write a short, engaging and interesting generating description for each product. Talk about its features and benefits. What sets it apart from other similar products? If there's an existing product description from the original merchant, you can simply seek their permission and copy their product description if it's effectively written.

Once you've uploaded all products, they will be presented in a list style layout, which can be modified. You can view the product image and its price. You also have the option of determining whether you want the product to be available to your fans.

Conclusion

"The secret of getting ahead is getting started."

- *Mark Twain*

Thank you for downloading *Facebook Marketing: A Comprehensive Guide for Building Authority, Creating Engagement and Making Money through Facebook.*

I genuinely hope this book was able to offer you lots of little tips, proven strategies and wisdom nuggets for building a powerful and profitable Facebook business.

I've tried to keep the techniques as straightforward and actionable as possible so even beginners can get their feet wet in the lucrative world of Facebook marketing.

The next step is to start applying these valuable tips immediately. Pick tips that work for you and work towards building a loyal community of buyers. At the end of the day, social media marketing is all about creating engagement, strengthening credibility, building strong brands, and eventually setting up a community of loyal buyers who turn out to be your most powerful evangelists.

Try different strategies and techniques, and pick the one that offers you the best results. You'll learn a lot of things along the course of your journey.

YouTube Marketing

–––––– ❧❧❧❧ ––––––

*A Comprehensive Guide for Building
Authority, Creating Engagement and
Making Money Through Facebook*

Mark Smith

Table of Contents

Additionally, the information in the following pages is intended only for informational purposes and should thus be thought of as universal. As befitting its nature, it is presented without assurance regarding its prolonged validity or interim quality. Trademarks that are mentioned are done without written consent and can in no way be considered an endorsement from the trademark holder.

Introduction

Congratulations on downloading this book and thank you for doing so.

The following chapters will discuss some of the basics that you need to know in order to get started with YouTube marketing. This is a form of marketing that some companies tend to overlook, but it is one of the best options that you can use to really form a relationship with your customers and promote your business. This book is going to spend some time talking about how to get started on YouTube marketing for your business.

There are so many things that you can do with YouTube that it is simply amazing. You don't want to just get started right away with a whole bunch of videos that will just talk about the product all the time. There is no connection here and your potential customers will get bored and quit following you. This book will not only show you how to make these sales videos later on down the line, but how to work on those first few videos so that you really impress the viewers and get them to stick around.

We will also talk about how you can provide value to your audience, how to really make those videos and the front page of your channel pop out, how to use analytics to figure out how well your videos are doing, and even how AdWords will help you to promote your site better than ever before. When all of these parts come together, it is really easy for you to get the views, and even the sales, that you would like.

When you are ready to see your business grow and you want to start adding some marketing with YouTube to the mix, make sure to check out this book. It has all the information that you need to make the right decisions and see an increase in sales in no time.

There are plenty of books on this subject on the market, thanks again for choosing this one! Every effort was made to ensure it is full of as much useful information as possible, please enjoy!

Chapter 1:

Getting Started with YouTube

Before we start looking at some of the cool marketing things that you can do with YouTube, it is important to get a good look at how YouTube works and how it got its start. This platform has such a huge audience with more than 800 million active users each month. This makes it the number one destination for browsing, searching, sharing, and promoting video content. When people want to see a video of something, whether it is about cooking, working out, how things are done, and so on, they are going to head to YouTube.

This means that YouTube is one of the most effective platforms that you can use to build up a big group of loyal followers, which are known as subscribers on this platform. Unlike some of the other social media platforms, like Facebook and Instagram, all the content that is placed on YouTube is going to be in a video format, making it very unique and personal.

Now, when it comes to marketing on YouTube, there are three pillars that are very critical. The first pillar is that you need to attract an audience to your channel through the videos you post. The better your videos, the more followers you will get.

The second pillar is that you need to engage the audience. Your audience needs to have some kind of involvement, emotionally or otherwise, with you or they will stop visiting. And the third pillar is that you need to upsell to your audience, which means that you should sell some kind of service or product to your audience.

All of these parts need to come together, through the videos that you create in order to help you to get the followers and the profit that you want. Now, some people may already have a business that has been successful on other social media platforms and now they want to move it to YouTube. You will be able to use these videos to promote your product, just make sure that the videos are not too full of sales, that they have some kind of hook that brings customers in, or you will lose out.

In other cases, you may be brand new to the business and want to promote yourself or get the business off the ground. This is just fine as well, you just have to find your angle as well. Remember that it is all about the connection that you make with the audience. There are millions of videos on YouTube so you need to figure out what will draw in your customers? What will make them pick you over another video and what will keep them coming back for more? Yes, it is fine to advertise your product and this is a great way to promote your company, but this can get stale and boring if it is all you show your customers.

So, let's say that you are ready to get going on YouTube. There are a few things that you should have in order first. First, you need to set up an account. This is pretty easy to do. If you already have a Gmail account, you should have it linked to YouTube and can use the same credentials to log on. If your email is already professional and you are comfortable using this to promote your business, you will be able to go onto your account and start.

Since most people have a personal email address and they want to use YouTube to promote their business, they may want to consider setting up a unique email address that is just for their business or just on this YouTube channel. This is pretty easy to set up. You simply need to go to gmail.com and set up the email and password that you want to use. From there, go through and get onto your YouTube channel to start.

From here you can set up some of your own settings. You can choose what language you use, some of the keywords that come with your channel, and even how you receive notifications. And of course, take the time to post a few videos to get the channel started (we will discuss how to get those first videos going and what needs to be in your video to make it stand out).

YouTube is a great place to form a connection with your customers and to make sure that you are able to sell your product in a way that other social media platforms are not able to do. This book will give you the answers that you need to get started and really build up that following in no time.

Benefits of marketing with YouTube

At this point, you may be wondering why you should take the time to market on YouTube. There are a lot of other sources for advertising that you can consider, so why would YouTube be one of the options that you put on your list. There are actually the number of reasons why YouTube can work so well, sometimes way better than the other avenues, and this can be true no matter what type of product or service you are trying to sell. Some of the benefits of working on YouTube include:

- It's free: while you will need to invest a bit of your time to figure out your target audience and to create the videos that you want to use, being able to upload and even make the videos that you want to upload will be completely free. What is another advertising source going to be free?

- Content is really powerful: in a world that is moving more and more online, content is king. And out of all this content, video content is some of the best. Many times people would rather watch information about a product or service online rather than read about it.

- Could go viral: if you make a video that is particularly good, emotional, funny, or something else, your video could have the potential to go viral in no time. What going viral means is that there could be thousands of people who will share your video with others they know. If it does really well, this could mean that your business is exposed to an infinite amount of people.

- Local and global audience: based on the types of keywords that you use, your video could be seen by people all over the world. You could even end up with clients from other countries if it all goes well. If you are worried about the reach going too far because you are just a local business, it is possible to change this so that you are only found by people in your region.

- Demonstrate your expertise: you can spend your videos giving away great tips, which help to show your viewers that you are the expert in your particular field. For many customers or clients that you are going after, they will have a choice between two businesses and you want to make sure that they pick you. If you have videos on

YouTube that show why you are a good choice, this will help your business to stand out.

- Selling all the time: just because you just spend a little bit of time on a video and then post it doesn't mean the work your video is doing is all done. Making a video is like one of the best salespeople in the world. You only have to make the video once and then load it to YouTube. Then the video can go to work, being available any time of the day or night that someone wants to take a look at it. And for each new video you create, you are making a new salesperson. There is really no limit to what you can do with this.

- Give them a face: sometimes what you need is to provide the customer with a face, a person they can trust, in order to form that connection to make the sale. And since it is impossible for you to go out there and meet all of your customers, creating a video that can do this work for you can really help If you are camera shy, you can make a video that is in PowerPoint and then add in a headshot so people can still see how you look.

- The video is very SEO friendly: this one is so important. When someone is doing a search online, it is likely that a video is going to hold onto a top spot during the organic searches. If this ends up being your video, this is a big deal because for one reason or another, and your hard work, your video is standing out above the other links. And of course, more people are going to see your video if it is ranked high in search results.

When it comes to marketing your business, there really isn't a site that is better than working with YouTube. This website will allow you to make some content that will connect with the customers and if you do the process right, which we will discuss more in later chapters, you are going to get some of the best conversion rates and sales ever.

Creating videos that do well

Of course, if you want to see some success on YouTube and do well, you need to make sure that you are creating some videos that will be popular on YouTube. Creating a good video can be tough. Some of the most popular videos that are available on this channel aren't particularly high quality, even though this is a feature that is recommended inside of your YouTube video, and some aren't all that unique. But they are still providing something of entertainment or value to the customer and so they are able to get a lot of views.

There are a few different factors that need to come into play when you create a video that is going to do well. You need to start out with a video that is high-quality as these are often going to do the best when you are working on a channel for your product or service. Try to make good videography, or hire someone who can, to help you get this.

You also need to add some value to the video. There needs to be some reason why people are going to choose to go with your video, and sit through and watch the whole thing, rather than moving on to something else. You need to be able to provide this value to your customers as much as possible. Figuring out how to add the value is the tough part since each company and product is going to be a bit different.

And you need to promote the video. If no one ever gets a chance to see your video because it gets lost on YouTube, it is going to be really hard to see your company do well. There are a few different methods of promotion that you are able to use, from AdWords and more.

Picking out keywords

While you work on your videos, you should be careful about the keywords that you use. This is going to be the best way to make sure that people are able to find your video when they are looking up topics similar to yours. There are many great keywords that you can choose from and pick the right ones can help you to find more viewers.

You should consider some of the things that your potential customers will look for when they need your product or service. What do the clients like to look up or what interests them the most? This is going to help you out quite a bit because it ensures that you are able to get the viewers that matter the most for you.

If you are not certain about which types of keywords you should use, think about

What is important to your users. There are also tools that you are able to use that help you pick out some of the best keywords. These really help you to reach your customers and get the viewers that you would like.

Adding value to the clients

No matter what kind of product you are selling or target audience you are trying to reach, you need to make sure that every video you create is adding some value to your customers. It is easy for someone who is new to the market to worry just about their own profits and making money, but if this kind of attitude starts to show up in your videos, and it will, you will never be able to get customers.

Your work should always be about what is best for the customer and one way to do this is to show the value of some kind to the customer. Even the videos that you do before you promote your product or service should be valuable to the customer. This can include entertainment value as well. If there isn't value to the customer in some way, they will not be willing to purchase it.

This is also where some of the relationship and connection between you and the customer will come into the picture. You want to create some videos that are going to not only do well but ones that help the customer feel like they are gaining value and becoming closer to you. When this happens they are much more likely to want to make a purchase from you later on when you start your conversion videos.

There are a lot of different ways that you are able to add some value to your customers. You can provide them with some entertainment value, something that will make them laugh or help them to feel emotional over your story. You can show them how the product will provide them some value in their daily lives (not just how the product works itself). Take a look at your product and some of the messages that you are trying to send out to the world, and you will be able to figure out the best way that your product is able to provide value to others.

Don't forget the promotion

You may have made the best YouTube video in the world, but without some promotion, it is unlikely that more than a few people are going to even look at the video You need to put in some effort to make a promotion work if you want to make some sales. The good news about YouTube is that there are millions of active viewers each month which means there are a lot of potentials. But it also means that there is going to be a lot of competition and if you don't do some promotion to help make your video stand out, it is going to end up lost in the crowd.

Since Google acquired YouTube recently, you will get the benefits of being able to use AdWords for Video to help you with this type of promotion. This is one of the best marketing and promotion tools that you can choose from. It has all the tools and you will be able to personalize things to reach the right target market, to stay within budget, and so much more. We will spend some more time talking about what AdWords is all about and even how to set up your own account.

You should really put this promotion to good use. Programs, especially AdWords, will be able to provide you with detailed information so you can see whether your work is paying off. You can see if you are reaching the right target market if you are seeing the conversion rates that you want and more. Never underestimate how these tools can work for you and use them to your full advantage.

No matter what kind of campaign you are trying to create, you need to use AdWords for Video on YouTube. But there are a few other methods that you can try out as well. Some people like to post their videos on Facebook. This is a good way to get some views because you can share with your friends and family, and ask them to share. If the video ends up being really good, you may end up with a video that goes viral.

Promotion is so important to help you see the results that you want with your video. Creating a marketing campaign can be a little bit scary, but it is the only way to figure out who you are advertising to and to make sure that your information is getting out to as many people as possible. There are a tons of great videos on YouTube that have never gotten any views before simply because the creators were too scared to run the promotion that they needed.

How well are you doing?

No matter what kind of product or service you are offering to other people, you need to make sure that you have some method in place that will help you determine if you are being successful or not. It is not good enough to just guess about this part because often you are going to be completely wrong. And since YouTube does have an analytics service available, why would you want to leave all of this to just guessing.

YouTube analytics will help you to keep track of what you are doing with your advertisements. You want to make sure that you are sending out the right message, that you are reaching the right kinds of people who would like to purchase your products and you want to make an impact with all of your hard work Using a tool like YouTube Analytics will help to make this happen.

There are quite a few options that you are able to choose when it comes to working on a marketing plan for your company. You can choose to work on advertising in print, radio, television, and even other social media sites. But nothing is as effective and unique as working with YouTube. This social media site will allow you to post videos, which really work in a unique way because they form a connection with you and the customer, something that is not always seen or possible with some of the other forms of advertisement that you want to work with. If you want to do something that is completely unique to your marketing campaign and reach a large group of people who will be interested in purchasing your products, it is time to start working on your very own YouTube campaign.

Chapter 2:

Doing Your First Video

One of the biggest challenges that new marketers are going to face is to get new users to their channel and looking at their videos. There are millions of videos on YouTube so standing out in the crowd can seem really hard at times. You need to be able to create a video that not only sells your market and your product but which will really attract people to view your videos.

So how are you going to make sure that these potential customers see your videos and find them in the crowd on YouTube? The answer to getting through this problem is to do traffic videos. These are developed, and then uploaded, by the content creators and they are able to reach a lot of customers in a short amount of time. The main purpose of these videos is to bring as many people into your channel so that they can see your value and the main content that you want to show to them.

These videos can be powerful because it will set the tone for your whole channel. These videos are going to be pretty short though; most of them will not be more than seven minutes long. They will appeal to a lot of people so the views will be high, but remember that these videos are not going to speak to everyone and only a few of these viewers are going to become your subscribers. But this is still a great way to get started and can help to bring your content to the top of search lists, which will help you out down the road.

There are a few different characterizations that you will find when you work on a traffic video. Some of these include

- Massive reach: these videos are going to have a very high count of viewers to help you get people to your channel.

- The audience that you bring in will be undefined, wide, and sporadic. This can bring in some people but a lot of times it will not bring too many viewers permanently.

- Short length: these videos usually won't be more than seven minutes long.

- High amount of likes,

- High amount of shares

- Lots of comments

- Low conversion rate to channel subscribers, but it can help you to get some more of the likes that you need later on.

So let's talk about some of the different types of traffic videos that you are able to try out in order to get people into your channel and looking at your content.

Viral videos

These types of videos are going to include some short clips that can end up getting tens of millions of views. This is usually because followers will share the videos on social media and other places. They will usually be unique so that they catch the attention of others and it increases the number of shares. It will also be a standalone video, which means there will not be other videos that go in this series.

The whole purpose of going with this kind of video is to get as much attention as possible and to promote sharing throughout the community. They don't really reach a specific demographic either but will appeal to a lot of different people through social media so you get as many views as possible.

There are a variety of topics that you are able to pick from for creating your viral videos. Some of the topics that work well include:

- Celebrities that are in unexpected situations

- Fights

- Accidents

- Spoof sketches

- Song covers

- Animal videos

- Pranks.

Trending videos

Another type of video that you can use to help promote your YouTube channel is trending videos. These are the videos that will be about current hot topics of trending topics throughout the world or in the media. These will also be standalone videos and they are meant to give a unique interest in social media in the hopes of reaching millions of people with just one video. Of course, this type of video is also going to be broad in terms of the audience that you reach, and there won't be a specific type of demographic.

There are a lot of great trending topics that you can use in these videos, you just need to watch the news and make sure that you keep up to date. Some of the topics that you can use for your videos include sports highlights, festivals after a movie, explaining new technology, movie trailers, and political elections.

General interest video

These videos are going to be on a topic that has a wide amount of interest so that most social media users would want to take a look at it. These won't be shared as much as some of the other options, but they will still get quite a bit of view because of direct searches. Sometimes they are known as Unintentional Virals.

Some of the topics that you can place in one of these general interest videos include tutorials, reactions, social experiments, and product reviews. They should provide some kind of information and value to your customers or the viewers so that you still get quite a few people viewing the information.

Collaboration videos

You will find that collaboration videos can be successful as well, but they will work in a different way compared to the other categories. In these videos, there will be a few different YouTubers who will come together in the same video, but they are all able to present their own content within that video. When each collaborator is done, each YouTuber who was in the video will share it on their personal channel, helping to cross-promote and reach a much larger audience.

To work on a collaboration video, you will need to find other channels who are similar to yours so that you can target the right users and share a message that is similar to all channels. This is much more targeted compared to some of the other options so you are more likely to get a higher conversion rate.

So how do you get one of these collaborations to work? You first need to make sure that you are showing value to the other people who would join in on the video. You should go through and find a few channels that have a similar content and amount of subscribers before getting started. Let them know that you enjoy their videos, that you have been watching them for a bit of time and that you find that their message is captivating.

Once you have made some contact, you are able to explain how collaboration is able to help both of you reach a bigger audience, get new users, and then expand out both of your channels. Remember that this is not just about you; there has to be some value between you and the other channels or you will not be able to get the results that you want.

Picking out the type of video that you want to use is sometimes the biggest challenge of getting your channel up and running. You have to pick out the type of video that would work the best and come up with a catchy idea that will get people to look at your channel and hopefully start to get some more likes and even more subscribers that will grow your business. This is going to be a great way to get started on your channel, but remember that there are other things that you have to work on as well.

Once the original viral video is up and running, you will need to work on creating some of the other videos that you want to have on your channel. These can be about your service and product and will help to bring some more of the targeted viewers that you would like to have, but the viral video can be a good way to help rank your channel and helps you to see results.

Chapter 3:

Understanding Your Audience

In the past chapter, we spent some time talking about one of the first things that you should do in order to attract some new users to your channel. The viral video is one of the best ways to get this done, but we still need to move on a bit more. The next task is to engage your viewers, the ones who found the channel in the first place and find a way to make them fall in love with your content. These are going to be your loyal customers, the ones that you will be able to upsell your services or products to later on. This is going to be the underlying process that will define your marketing on YouTube.

So the goal here is to produce content that is going to engage your audience. You need to be able to develop a thorough and deep understanding of who is in your target audience and what these people value. Before we begin though, there are two essential requirements that you need to keep in mind. When you are looking for an audience you must remember:

- The audience needs to have some interest in the subject or the theme of your videos.

- Your audience has to be active on YouTube

Now you will be able to identify your audience on YouTube. You have to remember that anyone you go after needs to fit into the two requirements that we listed above. If you have never spent much time working on marketing in the past, it may be hard to figure out how to pick out the right audience so that you can make some sales off your audience.

Before you start out on any of the videos that you want to create or you design your YouTube channel. You need to go through and answer these questions. These will help you to reach the right people and not waste all of the time and energy on reaching the wrong people. You should look back at the answers to these questions anytime that you are uncertain about what is going on or if you are sending out the right message to your customers. The five questions that you need to ask about your audience includes:

- How old are they? This can include whether they are teenagers or adults and even an age range if that helps.

- Where do these people live? Are they in a different time zone that will affect the time you post videos or are there any language barriers.

- Are they men or women?

- How do these people spend their day? Are they students, do they work, do they have families, and what is important to them?

- Why do these people go to YouTube for? How often do they go onto YouTube? Do they like to look for specific information when they are on YouTube or are they just passing time?

You will find that working with YouTube analytics, which will be discussed a bit more later on in this book, can be a great tool to help you pick out your viewers and learn more about them. Thanks to the fact that Google took over YouTube, you are now able to get details about the statistics of your viewers. In fact, you will be able to go through and see precise information about your viewers, and even more information about the audience as it grows. Or example, you are able to look through and see what type of information and content is going to appeal more to the women in your group.

If you have been in business for some time, you are going to be able to use some of the marketing information that you have used in the past. Your demographics can be similar on YouTube as they are on other social media channels so some of the work has been done for you. Of course, you have to remember that this social media is much different than some of the other sites. This one is going to rely just on videos, without copy and other words, so you may have to make some changes to reach your customers a bit better.

For those who are just beginning their process of marketing at all, you need to make sure that you do this analysis of your customers anyway. How are you supposed to make sure that you are marketing to the right people, rather than wasting your time and energy, no matter what type of marketing campaign that you are working on?

Knowing your audience is so important. You want to make sure that you are creating some great videos so that you reach your target audience and you don't waste your time and energy. By using the five questions above and asking as many other questions about your customers as possible, you will be able to get as much information in order as possible to create fantastic videos and make the sale.

Chapter 4:

Provide Value to Your Audience That They Can't Get Anywhere Else

The next part of this journey that you need to work on is how to provide value to your customers. It is not enough to just make a few videos and hope that people will like them. These videos need to be able to provide some sort of value to your customers, to solve a problem for them, to entertain them, or do something else. Just spouting out information about your product is not going to be enough to help keep the viewers around.

If you are interested in getting millions of people to look at your content, you need to make sure that the content is high in quality. The videos need to be way better than the competition, and there is a lot of competition that you will have to go against. If you want to make sure that you can attract some new viewers and keep your viewers around, you need to make sure that the videos are not only high quality but the content needs to provide value as well.

Value is something that you are going to hear around the marketing industry all the time, but very few people understand what this means. From a high-level perspective, it can be defined pretty easily. Basically, this value means that your audience is going to attribute a level of importance, worth, and usefulness to your content. However, it is going to be hard to figure out the exact value that your audience place on the video and content that you upload, especially since this industry is completely digital.

Let's look at an example of this. The Fail videos have become really popular throughout the web. These are basically stunted attempts that end up failing in unexpected ways and can lead to the person getting harmed quite a bit from the accident. FailArmy is a popular channel that has over 12 million subscribers.

But the real question here is how can you describe why people like these kinds of videos. The viewers are going to watch any content that is bringing them value and it is your role as the marketer of your company to identify the value of these videos and then maximize its delivery to you viewers. So why are the Fail videos so popular? They are not that high quality, they are definitely not original and they aren't that unique

There is an article that is found in Adweek took the time to discuss the Fail videos and why people like them so much. There are three factors that are discussed including the Ego stroke, the element of surprise, and the element of disbelief. If you want to launch a channel that is similar to the topics of fail videos, you will need to carry out a lot of research on these three elements so that you can add them into your videos and add in more engagement.

Figuring out what your viewer's value is really difficult. You are not able to meet the people who are watching your videos and you have to be able to figure out what these people like, what they do in their free time, what they enjoy or find interesting, and so much more. However, if you would like to see sales of your products, you have to be able to understand the value to your viewers.

From some of the other topics that we have discussed in this book, you should already have a good understanding of who your target audience is. If you don't already have this organized and figured out, you need to go through and do this right now before going any further. You need to have a good appreciation and idea of some features including their age ranges, their gender, the way they browse the internet, their lifestyle habits, and more. These insights are going to be really useful when it is time for you to understand what is going to be valuable to your customers when making your videos

In order to really develop this understanding of your audience, you can use the approach below:

Step 1: Assess the competition

When you first get started on your new YouTube channel, or any new business or marketing avenue for that matter, the first thing that you should do is take a look at your competition. It doesn't matter what you are trying to sell, there are going to be some sort of competition, or another channel, that you are going with on YouTube.

Having competition is important because this shows that there are market and audiences that are already around for your content. It is much easier for you to fill a market need than to try and create a new one. There are many different types of competition that you need to work with. The direct competition will be the people who are selling a product like yours or very similar. If you are selling jewelry, these would be the other people who sell jewelry as well.

But there will also be the indirect competition and you cannot forget about these people either. If you sell hamburgers and French fries, you will also want to compete with the grocery store, taco places, and other places to eat. Each company is going to have both direct and indirect competition so learning who these people are can really help you to make higher quality and more on target videos than your competition.

You should look at both the large and the small competitors within your field. The smaller ones are who you will work with right away, the focus you should have right now. The larger ones you can tackle later when you start to gain some steam.

To start, you should look at five of the small and five of the large channels that have similar objectives to you. For each of them, you need to pick out three parts of their channel that you really like. You can pick the behind-the-scenes cuts, the high-quality videos, the topics and more. Once you are done writing this down for all of them, it is time to go through and write down three aspects of the channels that you don't really like. Then on each of these points, you need to write down information on how you can solve the issue in your own channel.

While you are going through all of this information, you always need to think about why people are watching these videos? What are these viewers trying to get out of these videos? You can take some time to look at some of the comments because these will provide a lot of insight into how people like these videos. Remember that you should use the positives from your competition, but learn from the mistakes that they have.

Step 2: Refine and improve your value proposition list

In the past step, you were in charge of developing a list to describe why users are attracted to your competitor's channel. However, if you go through and copy the competition all the time, you are never going to see success. Instead, you need to work on improving it. You must be able to differentiate yourself in some way so that you can steal more market share and provide content that has better value.

In order to do this, you need to refine the value proposition list as described in the steps below:

- Compare the value proposition to the target audience profile you developed. Can you optimize any of these aspects to the gender, habits, and age range of your target audience?

- Always play to your own strengths. Do you or anyone on your team possess unique skills that are you are able to use? For example, if you are really good at Photoshopping, you can do this to make some really good videos.

- Produce content: once you are done with your value proposition, which you adopted in the previous step, now it is time to produce and add in some new launch videos on your channel.

- Evaluate: as you add some new videos on your site, you are going to start to get some more feedback. You can take this information and start it all over again. There are going to be times when you will experience some criticism, but it is important to not run from this information, but instead, go straight towards it and try to make some improvements. Yes, there will be times when the feedback is not all that useful, but other times when it could help you make big changes that will help you out.

One of the steps that you should work on is to isolate why some of your audience is positive to some of your videos and why they respond negatively to others. Once you come up with a theory, it is time to test the market. You can then start a new video that will address the customer feedback before going through the new response. Again, you will still get negative and positive feedback on the video (this will always happen because not everyone will like what you have to say), you can check out this new feedback and see if some new changes need to be done.

Continuous improvement is so important to help you see some of the results that you want. The companies that are dominating the market are the ones who always take a look at the feedback that you see on your videos and then you can make changes as needed.

Remember, in order to have a channel that is successful on YouTube, you have to first produce some content that is fantastic. But it is only one of the factors that you need to have come together to get the successful channel. Having high-quality videos can help you to attract some customers, but you need to have patience, learn how to engage your viewers, consistency, advertisement campaigns, and marketing in order to get the success that you want.

Chapter 5:

Tips and Strategies That Work

As we spent some time discussing earlier in this book, you need to take some time to know who is in your target audience, understand what they will value, and then be able to provide this to the right people. This is all so important for helping you engage your audience. However, it is important for you to remember that YouTube is a platform for sharing videos and it is going to rely on communication and on graphics, which means your content isn't the only thing that you should concentrate on.

There are a lot of different details that need to come into play when designing your videos. Just sitting in front of the camera and talking for a bit is not going to do the trick. Some of these include:

Graphics and appearance of the channel homepage

When viewers go to watch one of the videos that you post and they like it, it is likely that these people are going to visit your homepage. The branding and the graphics will be one of the first things that they notice, so they need to make a powerful impact. While there are a few different types of graphics that you can place on your homepage, but the two components that are the most important include:

The profile picture: this is going to be the image that is the most visible on your whole channel. It is going to appear in the videos and in all of the comments that you end up posting. Depending on the type of the business that you run, this could be a headshot of you or a company logo.

Banner picture: the banner picture is important as well. This banner picture is going to be a large one that is right in the background of your channel page. You want to make sure that this picture is of high-quality and that it is going to catch the attention of your viewers, helping to introduce them to the products or the subjects that you are promoting.

If you don't really have any experience with doing graphic design, it is a good idea to hire someone who can help you get this done. These graphics will be some of the first things that people notice when they go to your channel, so you want them to look nice. You will be able to find a few good designers to work with if you just search for a bit online. If you need some ideas of how your graphics should look, consider looking on some other channels to figure out what looks nice.

Banner video

Another thing that you need to work on is the banner video this will be the very first video that people will see when they come to your channel. You can have some fun with this kind of video, but you should make sure that it explains a bit about you, that it talks about your hopes for the channel, and even includes a bit of history about your business.

You do need to put some effort into this video because it needs to be one of your most engaging videos. It can only be a few minutes long, but it needs to be enough to convince someone who may have never heard about you in the past to like your videos and stick around. This needs to be a video that provides value to them and sell yourself.

Playlist and video arrangement

The playlist that you have on your channel can be a great way to attract new customers, but it does need to have some good groupings and the topics should be clear. You should have a structure that is effective or the channel. To start, you should write out a list of three or four topics that you think the viewers may enjoy, and then work to create your playlists around these subjects.

You do not want to end up with too many playlists when you first get started, so be careful when planning these out. You can add more of these later on, but as a beginner with just a few videos posted, it is best to start with just a few to keep things more organized. These are helpful because it is going to let a viewer know what your channel is all about right from the beginning and you are able to solve a problem for them this way, making things easier.

Engage right with the viewers.

No matter what type of product you are designing, you need to make sure that you and your viewers are working on a personal relationship. Your customers are interested in purchasing products from people that they know and trust so you need to work on this kind of relationship through the videos that you are creating.

There are a few strategies that you are able to work with in order to achieve a direct and strong emotional connection with all of your viewers. The first one is to learn how to speak right to your viewers and thank them for taking the time to look at your channel. The second thing that you are able to do is to be active in your comment section. While you may not be able to take the time to respond to everyone who is commenting on your videos, but making an effort and responding to as many of these as you can make a big difference.

As you can see, high-quality videos are so important when it comes to creating a great video to use on YouTube, there are some other factors that are so important to helping you to get views. You can make as many videos as you would like and post them, but without the other factors, you will get no views.

Chapter 6:

Upselling a Product or Service with the Conversion Video

So far in this book, we have spent some time talking about how to make up your viral video so that you can get people into your channel. Then we moved over to working on some videos that are going to connect with your viewers, things that will solve a problem and provide them with a bit of value in the process so they stick around. Now we are going to move onto the step that you need in order to start making money from your YouTube channel!

Once you have been able to funnel some more viewers to go to your channel and you have learned how to keep them engaged, it is time to learn how to sell the service or product that you have available. This one can be exciting because all of that hard work you have put into the rest of the process in order to start making the money that you would like.

Now it is time to convince the viewers that they need to purchase your service or product. In most cases, the viewers on your channel don't already have a need for the product. Otherwise, they would have just gone out and gotten the product already on their own. It is your job to show them how the product or the service is going to bring them value so they make the purchase.

One of the most effective ways that you are able to convince your viewers to go for your service or product is to use Conversion Videos. These types of videos are important because they are meant to convert the audience that you already have into customers. These videos can be longer in length, sometimes up to two hours although most companies will not make their videos that long.

It is important to remember that these videos are only going to appeal to a specific niche in your audience. You will not receive as many views on the video as you did and the comments and shares will be lower as well, but this is not a big deal. If you did the other steps correctly, you will still get customers to look at the video and they are more likely to be the ones you need to make the sale.

There are a few factors that you are going to be able to find in your conversion videos Some of the features that are found in these types of videos include:

- Longer video length that is often between five minutes and two hours.

- Low amount of shares

- Low amount of comments

- Low amount of likes

- A specific and refined audience

- Restricted reach that is pretty much limited to the subscribers you already have, so it is important to make sure that you have plenty of these in place before you start.

Now that we know a bit about these conversion videos, it is time to discuss some of the popular and most effective types of conversion videos.

Knowledge video

These videos are great because you will demonstrate an outstanding, complete, and extensive knowledge of a given topic. Your job on here is to show that you are an expert in your field, that you are the person that everyone else should go to if they want to learn more about this particular topic.

Through these videos, you are going to market out your knowledge in this field. This is going to help you to sell books, plans, advice, or something else. Often these are steeply priced so being able to show the subscribers that you have the value of working with you can be a big deal. Some of the examples of what can be shown in these knowledge videos include:

- Presentations and talks

- Personal opinions and podcasts

- How-to

- Tutorials

- Tips

Demonstration video

The next thing that you can work on is the demonstration video. This type of video is when you will show the viewers exactly how the product or service you are selling is going to work. Remember that the main challenge that you face when marketing a product is to show how your product or service will provide value to your customers. When you do a demonstration video, you are able to demonstrate to your customers how valuable the product is.

In these videos, it is more important for you to focus on the benefits that the product and service providers, rather than the way that the product works. Of course, you can show some of how the product works, but it is more important to show some of the benefits of this product. Some of the examples of how you are able to do this are with personal experience, product review, documentary, gameplay, testimonials, portfolio work, and client transformation.

Call-for-support video request

In these kinds of videos, you are going to need to work on the emotional bond that you have been building with your viewers. Even though the viewer may not necessarily need your product right now, you will find that these videos are perfect for getting them to make a purchase a form of appreciation for you and your videos. This strategy is only going to work out well for you if you have a lot of engagement from your viewers or an audience of millions.

You do not want to start with these conversion videos right off the bat. Your customers need to build up a relationship with you before they will make a purchase and if you just try to get them to make a purchase with the first video that you make, you are going to end up with some trouble making the sales that you would like.

But, if you start out with some relationship building videos first, videos that provide some sort of benefit to your customers and keeps them coming back for more, it is easier to use these conversion videos once your audience levels are up, so you can get the results that you want. You may be excited to start earning a lot of money right away when you are on YouTube, but if you don't appeal to your target market and give them some value ahead of time, you are putting in a lot of work for nothing.

Chapter 7:

Promoting Your Videos

Now, we have spent quite a bit of time in this book talking about how you can create videos and some of the different options that you can choose when you want to bring in more customers to your channel. So now that you have a great video, how are you going to promote your videos so that the most customers will see this content. You can have some fantastic videos and content to share with others, but without some promotion, you are going to end up with a lot of effort and nothing to show for it.

There are times, especially when you are just getting started on a new channel, where you are not going to be satisfied with how many views your video is able to get organically. Organic views are basically the number of users who are able to see and look at your videos without having to use paid advertising to help you out. For some people who haven't started with social media and online marketing, the idea of paying money for one of these marketing campaigns can seem a little bit overwhelming and expensive. The good news is that these campaigns can be really easy to do and if you create the right types of videos, it will easily pay for itself.

Although you may not realize it when you are on the other side of things, the channels that are the most successful on

YouTube are going to be the ones that use paid ad campaigns. But they don't just do a few little campaigns here or there; instead, they will do these on a big scale. For instance, some of the larger music videos are able to acquire their first two or more million through a big ad campaign that happens right after they release the video. Because of this and a large amount of traffic that happens right after the video has been released, the algorithm for YouTube is going to see this as an important video and will promote it. This means that YouTube will feature this video on their homepage and it can quickly go viral.

This means that using ads on YouTube is so important, but as a beginner, where are you supposed to start. This chapter is going to take some time to talk about which platforms you are able to use for advertising, what objectives you can achieve with each one, and even how to set up an ad campaign to help you get started.

The best tool in AdWords

AdWords is considered one of the best and largest advertisement services available online today. It is a service that is created and owned by Google and it earns more than $40 billion a year. Thanks to the amount of user information that Google has in their possession, AdWords will allow you to refine your target audience using interests, gender, and age. And after Google acquired YouTube, they also changed up AdWords so that it works with videos as well.

After being used for decades by many online advertisers to help reach their target customers, AdWords for Videos was developed to be used easily and to be accessible to everyone who would like to use it. All you need to do is create the ad that you would like to use, define the target audience, and then select your budgeting options. Once all of this is done, AdWords for Video will work to make sure that your ad is in front of any user that has looked at the similar content and will help you get more views and subscribers.

The question that most people have after all this information is how much does it cost to run a campaign with AdWords. You will be surprised at how inexpensive it is to place your content in front of an audience who is targeted, meaning an audience who is interested in the information and will likely follow your channel.

The nice thing about AdWords for Video is that you are only going to pay for the video once someone watches it. You won't have to pay just because someone sees the title of the video or anything else, but only when they actually take some time to look over your video. On top of that, if you are on a limited budget to get started, you are able to set a price per view or even a daily budget to help you stay on track.

If you find that the campaign is not working as well as you would like, or if it is doing better than you had hoped, you will be able to stop or modify your campaign at any time. You don't need to give up a notice to make this happen. Remember that both AdWords and YouTube offer sections for analytics so that you are able to see how successful all of your marketing campaigns are going to be, with a lot of precision to help you decide whether the campaign is doing what you would like.

Before you get started with any type of marketing campaign, much less one that you use with AdWords for your videos, you need to have an approach set up ahead of time and this approach needs to have some clearly defined goals to help you succeed. Another thing that you will enjoy about working with AdWords for Videos is that it is going to provide you with some settings that can help you to match the objectives of your campaign. There are quite a few of these available, but one of the three options below are often the best ones for a beginner to get started off:

- I want to reach more people: if you want to do a campaign that will reach a lot of people and funnel these people into your channel, AdWords is able to help you out with this. To help with objective, you will need to work on promoting a traffic video like the ones that we discussed earlier in this book.

- I want to increase engagement: if you want to do a campaign that will help to increase the engagement on your videos, you will find that there are some other tools that are more effective, but you can do a few things with AdWords. If you want to use AdWords for this, it is best to focus on the content, channel presentation, and quality before you move to doing this.

- I want to increase conversions: AdWords is one of the best tools to use for increasing conversions on your videos. Conversions are the number of people who end up purchasing the service or product that you promote on YouTube. You can work on increasing your audience members before starting and then promote these with an Upsell Video.

You will find that AdWords is going to make things so much easier. You will not be limited to just the subscribers that you are able to organically get into your videos. With the help of AdWords, you will be able to reach anyone who has expressed some interest in your services or products directly. Of course, most of these users will have no idea of who you are and that emotional connection is not going to be there. This sometimes results in a lower rate of conversion. But if you place the Upsell Video in front of enough people you will usually see an increase in your sales.

Advertising with Facebook

Although working with AdWords for Video is a great platform to use to advertise your channel, using Facebook is another channel that is available to help you out. Due to the large amount of personal information that people seem to share on Facebook, you will be able to effectively target audiences that you want to work with and show them your message.

If you are brand new to the marketing world and you want to keep your budget under control, working with Facebook is a great option for you. Many people see Facebook is one of the cheapest and most effective platforms for you to use for online advertisement. This is a good way to share some of the videos that you want to promote and get them to spread virally among your friends and others. You may need to do an advertising campaign to help spread this out beyond the few people that you know, but it can be a cost-effective way to bring people back to your YouTube channel.

Working with various social media platforms is one of the best ways that you can help to promote your video outside of YouTube. While that is outside the scope of this book, it can make a big difference in how many people will take a look at your videos and go back to your channel.

Chapter 8:

How to Create an AdWords Campaign

We spent some time talking about AdWords for Video on the last chapter and how it can be one of the best tools to help you get your content out to your potentials so that you can make money from your work. But if you have never worked on an AdWords campaign, it can be a little bit scary to get started on the first one. This chapter is going to split up the steps that you need in order to create your first campaign with the help of AdWords for Video. This process is really simple, even for people who are not used to doing an online campaign for their company.

The first step is to get onto the account for Google AdWords for Video This is going to help you to create your very own AdWords campaign. You just need to go to the website **www.adwords.google.com/videos**. You can use the credentials for your YouTube or Google account to get started. Then pick out your time zone and the currency you would prefer to use.

Once you have had the time to create your own AdWords account, it is time to link up your channel from YouTube and then create a brand new campaign. Before you are able to create this campaign, you need to make sure that you link together the AdWords account with your YouTube account. This makes it easier for you to select the videos you want to work with directly and it will provide you with campaign analytics that is more detailed. You can also use this to insert some call-to-action buttons if you would like. To start, you need to click on the "Linked YouTube Accounts" which is located right on the bottom left corner of the screen to have this happen.

Once you are on that link, it is time to create a new campaign. You need to look for the button that is called "All Video Campaigns". You will be able to find this on the top left corner of the screen. When you have found that button, you will be able to choose "+New Video Campaign" to get started with the first campaign.

You will want to select a few parameters that you would like to have on your campaign to make it look nice the first parameter that you should set for this campaign is what you would like to call the campaign. Make it something catchy and easy to remember so you can find it later on. And the second parameter that you need to set is the daily budget you would like to spend. This can help you to keep things under control and that your budget won't reach to the sky.

While you are setting up the parameters that you want to use, it is time to work on defining the location and languages that come with your ad. You can first start by refining your audience and who you would like to reach you can choose which cities the audience lives in and even the country if you would like to expand out the audience a little bit. And of course, make sure to pick out the language that will reach your target audience the most.

Once some of the parameters are set for your ad, it is time to pick out the video that you would like to show up when the ad is displayed. In order to get this started, you need to look for the button that says "select video" and then search through the list of available videos to find the one that you want to display. You can also do this by using the URL link, the channel name, or the keywords to make this easier. You will want to make sure that the video you are promoting is one that will capture the attention of your customers and bring them in to get more views. Use some of the tips in the first few chapters to figure out which one you would like to use.

When you are working with AdWords for Video, you will find that this program is going to use TrueView. This is a marketing model that is only going to charge the advertiser when a viewer has actively watched your video ad. There are a few formats that you are able to choose when you create your TrueView ads, and these are going to determine where the ad is going to be displayed on the page on YouTube. It is important to pick the one that is best for you to ensure that you will be able to get the results that you want. The four formats that you can choose for TrueView include:

- In-search: this is where the ads are going to appear on the search page for YouTube. Viewers will be able to see the ad, either next to or above the search returns on YouTube when they start to search for content that is related to your video. You will only need to pay when someone clicks on the ad and then watches your video.

- In-display: with this option, your ads are going to appear right next to the videos on the watch page on YouTube. Viewers will be able to click on your display ad in order to watch the video that is in the ad or on a YouTube watch or channel page. This one is also where you will only pay when someone clicks on the ad and then watches the video.

- In-stream: this is when the ads are going to play pre-, mid-, or post-roll on one of the YouTube partner videos that can be of any length. With these, you can place a whole ad, but the viewers do have the option to skip away from your video after five seconds are done. You will only have to pay for the ad when someone watches the entirety of the ad or after 30 seconds are over.

- In-slate: this is when the ads are going to play before a partner video on YouTube. Usually, the videos that the ad will play before will last over ten minutes. Before the video plays, the viewers will be able to choose to watch one out of three ads, or they will be able to watch regular commercial breaks throughout the video. You will only need to pay when someone clicks on the ad and starts to watch the video.

As you can see, there are different amounts of exposure that you will be able to get when you choose each of the options. Some will not get as many views as others but will be cheaper than the other options or you can get more views and pay a bit more. It is all about what you would like to do to target your customers and how much your budget is to do this.

Once you have chosen the type of ad that you would like to do from the formats that were above, it is time to define how you would like the ad to appear to your viewers. The main features that you need to spend time defining include the text of the headline, the description text, the destination URL, the thumbnail image, and the name of the ad (this last part is only going to be seen by you and the viewers will never see it).

At this point, it is time for you to set your own target bid. This is the section where you are going to be able to define the most that you will be willing to pay for each add. You will notice that this is called the CPV or the Cost Per View. Remember, that in most platforms online and social media, ad space is going to be assigned based on a bidding strategy. If you end up sending out bids that are too low, you will not be able to win any space for your ad.

There are a few different bidding settings that you will be able to pick out when it comes to this process. You are able to choose between the basic bidding settings or the advanced settings. The advanced bidding will make it easier for you to make modifications to the bid for each of those four ad locations we talked about before, whereas, in the basic bidding, you are going to maintain the same maximum bid no matter which ad location you are using.

Next, you will need to name and then save the target audience you would like to work with. This is not something that the viewers are going to be able to see, but it can help you to keep things organized in this campaign and will be nice for your future campaigns. From here, you will be able to proceed and then define who the viewers of your ad campaign are, also known as defining your target audience.

You will be asked during this process to pick out some keywords as well. You want to pick out some keywords that are relevant to the users you are working with. This makes it easier for them to find you when they do a search similar to what you are offering. If you are having trouble coming up with the keywords that you would like to use, you should just do a quick search for the interests that your audience has. You can also use the service known as "Get Targeting Suggestions" from YouTube so that you can pick out the audience you want to work with and then see the keywords that are the most relevant.

It is possible to use the same kind of process in order to select targeting keywords that are negative. These are going to represent the users that you do not, under any circumstances, want to advertise to. For instance, if you are working on a channel that really promotes barbecue meat, you may want to pick out a negative target keyword for the word "vegetarian."

And finally, you need to make sure that in this last section you are providing the right payment information to AdWords. Your ads will never be published on YouTube if you do not provide this payment information because YouTube wants to get paid when you get views.

Working with AdWords is not a complicated process, even though we did take a few pages to go through it all You will see that there are a lot of suggestions and modifications that you can make, but this is all meant to make things easier for you to target the right people. Take the time to consider the best placement for your ads on YouTube, the right keywords, the video you want to use, and so on, and you are more likely to get the results that you want to form these targeted campaigns with AdWords.

Chapter 9:

Tracking Your Performance with the Help of YouTube Analytics

Once you are done creating your campaign with all of the tools that we have talked about so far in this book, it is time to move on to figuring out whether the campaign is working or not. No marketer wants to get into the game and hope that things will work out for them, but never really having a way to find out whether they are reaching the right audience or not. This is where YouTube Analytics can come into play.

YouTube Analytics is a tool that will provide you with a lot of information on the success and the growth of your audience, videos, and the whole of your YouTube channel. If you have never used something like YouTube Analytics before, you are going to be shocked at all of the information that is provided inside of this tool once you get started. For example, it is possible to use this tool to find out exactly how your audience reached your YouTube channel, right down to the link that they clicked on to get to you. This is just one of the cool things that you are able to do with YouTube Analytics.

How to access YouTube Analytics

While YouTube Analytics is a great tool to use, you have to make sure that you are able to access it before you are able to use it to your advantage. On some social media platforms, you will find that it is difficult to access the analytics tools that they have set up. For example, you are only able to get access to the analytics that is available on Twitter if you pay for marketing campaigns through them. The good news is that getting onto YouTube Analytics is free and pretty simple.

The first step that you need to do is log onto your personal YouTube channel. Once you are there, you just need to follow the link **www.youtube.com/analytics**. After you have had time to open up this page, you should search for the tool bar. There should be an Analytics tab that you can click on before being sent over to the overview section.

The overview screen is a good place to start. It is going to provide you with a summary of the most important relevant data that is on your channel. You can just glance through this page and get some of the general trends of your channel. There are going to be quite a few items that will be listed in this overview screen. Some of these include:

- View reports: this is the place where you should go if you would like to figure out the number of views that you have received over time. You can also use it to see the source of all these reports to target your advertising better.

- Demographics report: with this tab, you will get a good breakdown of your audience. You are going to use this data to refine the profile for the target audience that we made earlier in the book. Some of the most relevant metrics that you will find include age breakdown, playback location, and gender distribution.

- Traffic sources report: this is a really important report that you will be able to use. It is going to help you to learn exactly how a user found your video, which can be so important when you want to grow your channel. For example, if an external blog featured your video, you will be able to see how many of your views came from that particular source.

- Audience retention report: this is going to be the most important data to engage your audience. It is going to show you how well the audience was engaged during the whole video. Often engagement is going to fall off as the video goes on unless something amazing is going on during your video. It is important to figure out where you are losing the audience and use this as a method to improve your video.

After you get started with a new video or a new ad campaign, you should give it a little bit of time to get out there and for people to take a look at it. You will not be able to get very good analytics half an hour after you post a brand-new video. The good news is that you will be able to get some good updates on a regular basis if you are patient and let the analytics do their job.

It is a good idea to go through this analytics on a regular basis so that you can get things set up and ready to go in a timely manner. There is so much information that you will be able to get from this analytics and you can use this information to figure out the best topics to work with, the best places to advertise, and so much more. Remember that your videos need to provide some form of value to the viewers so if you see that engagement is dropping off or you are not getting the number of views that you would like, it may be time to switch things up a little bit. Analytics will help you to get this done so you can see the results in no time.

Conclusion

Thank for making it through to the end of this book, let's hope it was informative and able to provide you with all of the tools you need to achieve your goals whatever they may be.

The next step is to figure out exactly how you want to sell yourself on YouTube. The type of product that you have for sale is going to make a huge difference in this, so be prepared and working on that first video, the one that is going to draw people in can often be one of the best places for you to get started. Many people are too worried about making videos that are going to just sell their products, but they forget that the customers want to feel a bond with the seller first, long before they look at any of the products that are for sale.

This book has all the information that you need to get started with success on your own YouTube channel. It doesn't matter what kind of product or service you are trying to sell, you want to make sure that you are following the steps that we outlined. From understanding how to make your first video to providing value to your customers, to a promotion of the videos, and even to promoting your own product over time, you will gain all the insight that you need to see results with this unique form of marketing.

YouTube is not a marketing channel that you want to turn down. There are so many things that you will be able to do with this channel and it is so effective at helping you to form that relationship with your potential customers. When you are ready to get started with using YouTube for your marketing needs, make sure to read through this book and learn everything that you need to know!

Instagram Marketing

$--- -- \prec\!\!\!\sim\!\!\!\ll\!\!\!\gg\!\!\!\sim\!\!\!\succ --- --$

A Picture Perfect Way to Strike It Rich!

Mark Smith

Additionally, the information found on the following pages is intended for informational purposes only and should thus be considered, universal. As befitting its nature, the information presented is without assurance regarding its continued validity or interim quality. Trademarks that mentioned are done without written consent and can in no way be considered an endorsement from the trademark holder.

Table of Contents

Introduction

Congratulations on downloading *Instagram Marketing: A Picture Perfect Way to Strike It Rich!* and thank you for doing so! We know that there are a lot of books out there about technology and social media, and we are really glad that you chose ours! In case you haven't noticed, technology is rapidly taking over the world. Chances are, more than half the people around you are on their cell phone or laptop at this moment. People no longer send mail by the postal service, rather they send a nice little text to a friend. Some people no longer buy clothes and shoes at malls, but rather on Amazon. The truth is that the smartest businesses have already taken notice of this and are plotting to maximize profit by using technology to sell their products. This book is going to teach you about marketing on one type of social media website that is increasingly popular - *Instagram.* If you take note of our tips, we bet that you will get your brand out there and increase your sales in no time!

First and foremost, the following chapters are going to share with you why technology is so important in today's world. They will introduce *Instagram,* a social networking app with more than seven hundred million users. From then on, you will learn the basics of creating a separate business account on Instagram and master the tricks that will help you interact with your potential new customers. You will know about the different communities on Instagram and learn how to direct your advertisements at people who will be the most responsive to your business.

Not only that, but you will also learn how to navigate the world of paid advertising and successfully blend in your ads with everyone else's normal posts. This book will show you how to do basic photo and video editing so that you can refine how your product looks in a picture.

Finally, we will show you how to use Instagram's "Insight" tools so that you will be able to see what type of person is attracted to your product or services and target towards that type of audience. We will show you how to use your location to communicate with locals near your small business, and we will make it a big success in your area when it comes to advertising!

There are so many books out there about using social media to your advantage, but thank you so much for choosing this book! We hope that you find this book both an enjoyable and useful read, and we bet that you will improve your business once you put our tips to practice!

Chapter 1:

Why Instagram?

A Blast from the Past!

As you may have noticed, the world around us is constantly changing. Just the cell phone in itself has gone from a screen larger than your personal laptop to the small smartphones that we have today. Yeah, sure, it might not be *exactly* what Back to the Future predicted, but it's really not far off. Day by day, technology is vastly altering our lifestyle. We communicate with emojis, order Starbucks on our phone to skip the line and buy all of the season's newest trends online. People "scroll down the feed" to see pictures of elementary school friends, "like" our parents' Facebook statuses, and "share" the coolest memes with our internet friends. It is easy to forget that without the world of social media, we wouldn't have any of these conveniences.

Don't Know Much About History...

There have been prototypes of computers around since the 1940s, but nothing was fast enough to get anything done back then. Mainstream computers have been around since the 1960s, but there weren't many uses outside of conventional programming. In the 1990s, Tim Berners-Lee changed it all. He set off a new flame in the world of computers by inventing the World Wide Web, or what we know as "The Internet." Not long after, social media was born, with the first notable one, *Six Degrees,* debuting in 1996. Because of this, people began to share ideas and photographs with others who were halfway around the world and connect with long lost friends who were ten thousand miles away. The early 2000s saw the rise of *Myspace* and *AOL chat rooms,* and after *Facebook and Twitter* exploded in 2006, everyone was hooked onto some form of social media. Smartphones only fueled this fire, and suddenly, people far away from us in location were just a click away. Even though these social media websites were a huge success, a lot of them felt like a chapter book that was too long - there were only words and no pictures. Sure, there were profile pictures, but the main focus of a social media page was never on photos or videos. On October 6th, 2010, two friends in San Francisco, Mike Krieger and Kevin Systrom, changed the face of social media forever. that day at midnight, they launched their new app, *Instagram.* A combination of the words "instant camera" and "telegram," the new social media app *Instagram* allowed its users to share the most defining moments of their lives with their friends online. The app was a huge success. In just a month, two million people were using the app. Facebook acquired the app in 2012 and they are still constantly improving its functions. Today, one of their features even surpasses The use of *Snapchat.*

Now, What Does This Social Media Crap Have to Do with My Small Business?

The world of a businessman is fairly simple. You simply figure out where potential customers are and advertise your product or service there. As you can clearly see, people in developed first world countries probably use the Internet more than they leave their house. Ever since Instagram's launch, many businesses have begun to take notice of that, implementing the popular social media website into their marketing system. It's easy to use, and that has made it a clever advertising tool for so many different organizations! More than five million businesses worldwide, including *McDonald's* and *Lays Potato Chips,* have hopped onto the Instagram bandwagon in order to increase interest in their products and find the right people to market to. With Instagram, many businesses do not even pay one single cent to get their products advertised if they know how to market the right way.

Shoot... How do I do this?

The business aspect of Instagram is very different from a personal account that you use to talk to your friends. The first thing you should do is sign up for an Instagram Business profile, separate from your other accounts. The good news is that although promoting advertisements requires a little bit of money, signing up for a so called "business" or "professional" account is completely free! Here is how you can sign up for an Instagram business account!

Step One: **Download the App!**

This really is only a good idea if you have a smartphone. The first step to starting your profile is having the means to do it in the first place! If you own an iPhone, head to the Apple Store, and if you own an Android, go to the Google Play Store to get the free app! Once it has finished installing, open the app!

Step Two: **Make Sure that You Have a Working Business Email Address**

It is easier to receive updates from the possible clients or partner businesses that you are following through email if you separate it from your personal one. Also, each account requires an email address that it is associated with. The good part about linking up a business email is that you can find all of your work contacts (co-workers, customers, and bosses that you keep in touch with) fairly easily through the "Find Friends" function on Instagram. Alternatively, you can provide Instagram with a phone number instead, if it is not already linked to another account that you have if you happen to have more people from work in your phone's contacts.

Step Three: **Open the App and Press *Sign Up***

Use the email you just created or the new phone number that you have.

Step Four: **Enter the Right Contact Information (and Double Check if It's Correct)**

It's okay to enter your actual first and last name. You can switch to a Business Profile once you have your actual account created.

Step Five: **Pick a Profile Picture**

You HAVE to be strategic about this. There will be a +Photo button on the page. Click on it to add your picture. Make sure that this is a picture that you can recognize even from the small thumbnail, and be sure that it is relevant to your company. A good picture to use would probably be your company's logo if you have one, or maybe a mascot of your company. It's best to avoid your own personal picture because that represents you more than it represents the company.

Step Six: **Choose a Relevant Username**

This can be the name of your company, or it could be something that represents your company. You want to make sure that it is easy to find. When other people search your business on the search engine, you want them to be able to find your official business account.

Step Seven: **Link Your Facebook Account and Find People to Follow**

Instagram will want you to link your Facebook account so that you can connect with the people that you already know. Keep in mind that in order to switch any account to a business account, it requires a Facebook account as well, so be sure you link it to Facebook, either your business one or your personal one! Now, you can follow the Facebook friends that are affiliated with your business as well.

Step Eight: **Confirm Your Email!**

A lot of Instagram's functions are disabled if they do not know that your email actually belongs to you, so be sure to go to whatever email you linked it with and verify that it is your true email.

Step Nine: **Now that You Are Actually in the App with a Functioning Account, Change to a Business Profile!**

On the bottom of your screen, you will see a bar on the bottom with five icons. The first one is your home page. The second one is to search for more users, and the third one is to post. The fourth one lets you see your activity, while the last one with your profile picture on it lets you see your actual profile. Beside "Edit Profile," there is a small icon that looks like a wheel. Press that button and scroll down. Underneath "Blocked Users," you will see a button that says "Switch to Business Profile." Press that, and you are on your way to get started!

Step Ten: **Enter Your Address When You Are Asked for it, and Your Business Email and Business Phone Number as Well**

There will be a "Contact" button on your profile for those that want to ask you questions, and this is the easiest way to let them know how to reach you!

Step Eleven: **Make Your First Post!**

Now that you have all the basics set up, you are only one post away from starting an adventure of a lifetime! You will be able to cultivate and grow your business all on social media now. Make sure your first post introduces your business and entices potential customers! You could take a picture of your business building, a product that you feel like everyone would love, or even members of your crew!

Step Twelve: **Share that First Post with Other Social Media Websites Like Facebook and Twitter!**

Press the three dots beneath your picture comments once you have made your first post! You will find there that you will be able to connect your Instagram post with so many other popular social networking websites, increasing your potential fan base! Now that you have started posting, check the heart icon on the bottom bar in order to see who has liked your post, followed you, or even mentioned you!

Once you have the account, make sure you manage it daily and check your Direct Messages mailbox located on the top right corner just in case anyone wants to ask you any questions. You can let your close friends know about the account, and they can help attract more people to the page by following it. Congratulations!

Now that this is done, we are going to show you how to exploit the natural benefits that social media comes with. You do not have to pay Instagram in order to get new people to know about your business - you simply have to know how to find people who are interested and keep them enticed. The next chapter will make you and everyone else in your business the newest social butterfly on the block!

Chapter 2:

YOU Are Instagram's Newest Social Butterfly: Ways to Connect with New Customers that You Never Would Have Thought About!

Now that you know all about the new world of Instagram and the basics of creating an account, it is time for you to learn how to make the most out of this app without spending a single cent. Paid advertisements are not the only way to succeed! You're probably wondering how you can successfully pick the right people to market to and rack in a lot of cash, so here are some foolproof ways that can help you increase your audience in seconds...

Make Sure Your Biography/Contact Information Is Correct

Before people will even look at all your posts, they will judge you by how you present yourself on your profile page. For business accounts, it is crucial that you have all your contact information right - that means name, address, phone number, and everything. If people try to contact you and cannot find you, they will get mad. In addition, be sure you have a convincing biography sentence that describes exactly what you do. It is a bonus if you can make it catchy as well. You need to explain what your brand or company offers and make it clear. Next up, have a link to your own personal website included. All of this can be changed with the "Edit Profile" button on your profile.

Finding Accounts with A Similar Niche/Common Interest And Interacting with Them

On your Instagram app, there is a bottom toolbar of five functions. Click on the magnifying glass, which is the second icon from the left. This is your "Explore" page. You can use the search engine to look for businesses similar to yours, go to their followers, and follow those people in order to gain attention. For example, if you are a daycare business, you can look up parenting clubs in your town and follow the people who are liking those posts. You will likely reach someone who is interested in your business or services. You can also message these people and send them special deals for your business through your Instagram Business account. The possibilities are endless, which brings me to my next topic. Once you find these people, it is easy to start a "Share for Share" campaign with a partner business.

Share for Share

Once you create your account and make posts, there are bound to be people who like your posts and/or comment on them. Reach out to those people and message them, asking them if they would like to share a post promoting your account in exchange for you doing the same for their business. Most of the time, underground businesses or businesses that have not gotten too big yet will agree to do this for you. This is like having an advertisement that is paid without actually paying for it. Your best bet is finding another account with a similar follower count (For example, if you are just starting out and have a hundred followers, find another account with a hundred followers as well). that will increase the chances of them saying yes to you. You can ask them to share your post through a comment on their page or a Direct Message (the mailbox on the top right corner of your Instagram app). Share for Share increases the publicity of your page and may even help you get a partner business.

Shout Outs

A shout out is a post thanking a customer for something they have done! If you see someone in your store buy a lot of your products and they do not mind being photographed in front of the store or being mentioned on Instagram, feel free to take a picture of them, upload it, and thank them for their business! Mention their name on the account! A lot of customers will appreciate that you actually took the time out of your busy schedule to get to know them and pay attention to them.

Kickstart Your Business With The Newest Trend: Hashtagging!

What are hashtags and why should I use them?

You may be asking what a hashtag is, or you may have already heard of it. After all, a couple did name their baby girl Hashtag in 2012. They were first used on Twitter, but they have moved over to Instagram as well. Hashtags are any word that follows a "#" sign (the hash or pound sign) that puts a post in a category. For instance, an ice cream shop owner might use the simple hashtag #food to get attention, and the CEO of American Eagle might make a newly branded hashtag like #AEO (American Eagle Outfitters) to represent their company. Hashtags can be put in the captions of Instagram posts so that people can search up posts in the category that they want to look at. According to a "Simply Measured" experiment and study, posts get 12.6% more activity when hashtags are used! There are strategic ways to use hashtags, and we are going to show you how to use them!

What are the different types of hashtags that I can use?

Brand Name (Branded) Hashtags

I know that most people would suggest that you pick a hashtag that is currently trending or popular, but brand name hashtags stick in your potential customers' heads and help them remember you. There are a few tips that will help you create a memorable hashtag. First, the suggestion is that you keep it short and to the point. You do not want to use any really complicated vocabulary words that will make your customers mistype your hashtag while posting anything themselves, so make sure that you use words that are both easy to remember and spell! Once you have decided on a hashtag name, you can use this on Instagram and many other social media web pages.

An example of a brand name hashtag is Coke's #ShareACoke campaign. Honestly, anyone who has been paying attention to the food community on Instagram probably knows about this hashtag since it is so simple and memorable. When Coke released the "Share A Coke" labels on all their bottles and cans, they created this hashtag so that friends could show each other online whenever they found a drink with the other person's name. Not long after, people started posting a lot of pictures of Cokes, thus helping the company advertise without spending any extra money! This hashtag is the perfect example of both a relevant and simple tag that many people can remember. Even today, many years after its release, people are still using this hashtag to post artsy Coke drinks on their profile. Just their posts may make you want to go grab a Coke now!

Brand name hashtags are good if you have a creative idea and want to keep a tagline that makes you stand out in the crowd, but like everything else, you always have the option of using another type of hashtag. You might want to consider creating another hashtag if you want to link it to a discount, contest, or another campaign.

Campaign and Contest Hashtags - Free Stuff and Free Publicity Attracts SO Many Customers!

You can also interact with your followers and get them to share your product on the internet by making a campaign hashtag. Campaigns or contests are often hosted by a small business or a big name brand in order to get attention. Prizes can vary - it can be a sample of your product, a cash prize, or maybe just the chance to be featured on your website provided that you have enough followers. This not only allows you to get your brand out there, but it creates a sense of community between all of your fans!

A good example of this type of hashtag is Ben and Jerry's "Capture Euphoria" campaign that they launched back in 2012. With hundreds of thousands of followers, the chain ice cream restaurant used #captureeuphoria to unite ice cream fans around the world. The idea is to take a unique picture with your ice cream (whether it be a selfie or one of someone else) and to upload it to Instagram and share your happiness eating ice cream with the rest of the world. By using that hashtag, the people who participated automatically got their picture uploaded onto a huge photo gallery website. The best ones got featured on the official Ben and Jerry's Instagram and local newspapers. The twenty best pictures got displayed on their professional advertisement! Though this contest did not have a monetary award, people who loved to get their picture featured participated - both buying an ice cream from their company and advertising online for all their friends to see! You simply have to come up with a contest and make a post, and your followers will do all the work for you!

Next, we'll discuss another type of hashtag that you may be more familiar with.

Trending Hashtags - Hashtags Dependent on Special Occasions, the Season or Date, and Etc.

Trending hashtags are simple. They are simply hashtags popular for a specific day! For instance, if you were selling American flag print bikinis for the Fourth of July, you could try to promote your post with the hashtag #4thOfJuly a week before the holiday. A popular example of this is #SelfieSunday. On the internet, many teenagers and adults alike love to post a selfie of themselves on a Sunday using this hashtag. If you are a clothing business, you can use this to your advantage by including it in your caption so those people that like to look at different people's Sunday selfies can find you as well. It is not a good idea to only use these hashtags because often, many people are using them and it will be hard to find your post even ten minutes after you post it. However, it isn't much extra work to maybe add just one of these on to the end of your caption. Who knows, even one extra person viewing your post is still extra publicity for you.

Common, Everyday Hashtags and Their Uses

There are also hashtags that everyone else uses. These are the hashtags that are not exclusive to businesses, such as #coffee or #yoga. Though these hash tags may not gain you much publicity because of a number of people looking at it, it may still reach a few people. However, as a business, you must know that people craving the type of product you sell may be looking at these hashtags to see what choices they have. For instance, if you are a local coffee shop, you can take a picture of your famous mocha and use #mocha to attract more coffee drinkers.

This Is Especially Important for Small Businesses - Use Geographical Hashtags to Your Advantage!

Even if you live in a place, you still may not know about every little business in the area. Luckily, by hashtagging whatever place or city your business is in, customers have a greater chance of finding your shop when they need your particular service. For instance, if you live in New York City and have a computer shop there, you can use #NYC and make a post about your services so that locals know where you are in the middle of a busy, crowded city. The minute locals know about your business and fall in love with your services, they will gossip to their friends and spread your name out there in your community. The money comes rolling in.

So How Do I Find Popular Hashtags to Use?

Use the "Explore" page on your Instagram (second item on bottom toolbar" to research posts similar to yours. This whole page generates posts for you to look at based on the people that you follow, the posts that you like, and the people that interact with you on Instagram. Here, you can find the hashtags that businesses around you are using and the hashtags that people selling similar products are using. The truth is, researching what hashtags your competitors are using will not only help you figure out how many hashtags to use and which ones, but it also provides a chance for you to look at someone else's product and figure out how yours can be better.

How Do I See if My Hashtag Is Doing Well?

When someone posts a caption with a hashtag, the hashtag always appears in blue font rather than a black font. This is because it is a link. Once you click on the hash tagged word, you can see every post that involves that hashtag! This is very useful if you are tracking a hashtag you created specifically for your brand or a contest.

How Many Hashtags can I Use?

You can use as many as you want! Many people will use around one to five to avoid "spamming" with a hashtag.

Hashtags are a way to increase visibility and attract people with a common interest to your business, all at no cost at all!

Mentioning, Tagging, and Direct Messaging (Otherwise Known as DMing): Let Your Fans and Partners Know that You Are Noticing Them!

Now that we are on the topic of captions (with hash tagging), it is also worth noting that "mentioning" or "tagging" your followers on your posts can increase your visibility and make you more approachable as a business.

While posting a picture, there is an option called "Tag People." Here, you are returned back to your picture and you can press on a face or an object to tag another account, thus letting them know that you have posted. You can tag people in photos and tag loyal customers in a post about a product. The choice is yours, but this tool allows you to show everyone else the people related to your post.

Mentioning is also another choice that you can make as an Instagram marketer. While writing a caption or commenting on either your own post or someone else's post, you can press the "@" key and follow it up with someone's username to mention them. This can allow you to notify other people that you are needing to say something to them!

Finally, there is a small icon near the top right corner of your screen called the "Direct Message" icon. You can use this function to privately message anyone of your choice. You can use this to discuss business with partner companies or to answer questions that loyal customers or new people have.

Instagram Live: It's Like TV, But It's Just for Your Business

How would you like it if people could look at what your business is doing at a specific set time, or if your business could have its own little show just like *The Bachelorette* or *Grey's Anatomy?* This is all made possible with a 2016 addition to Instagram called Instagram Live. By swiping left and then switching to the "live" option, you can create and stream a video with all your followers. Instagram will notify all of your followers that you are going live. While you are streaming, the people who are watching your video can comment their opinions or questions and like what you are doing. Now you're probably wondering why you need to go live to advertise your business. For one, it increases your visibility/publicity and makes your business stand out against competitors. You can also get more up close and personal with those that follow you. There are plenty of things you can do with the Instagram Live feature!

Here are some things that you should probably do before you start an Instagram Live video:

- Know the information about your company. If someone asks you a question, you want to be able to answer it fully. If you have a knowledgeable employee at your business, they can take over this job as well. Know your products inside and out!

- Dress more professionally so people take you seriously.

- Advertise before the session! Make posts or promote the session to people you know who live around you. You don't want to start a live session, reserve that time out, and then have nobody show up.

- If it is a tutorial on how to do something or a tour around your business, practice! Treat this as if you were giving a public speech to thousands of people because that is basically what you are doing (except over the Internet). Remember that you are your business' representative when you are going live!

Now, here are some ways to take advantage of the tool...

Start Question and Answer Sessions and Ask Customers What They Want

The magic of Instagram Live is that it allows you to connect with your fans or followers on a face to face basis. This means that you do not have to go through all the nonsense of emailing, texting, calling, or sending people videos and pictures just to answer one question. They can comment the question on your live session, and you can answer them right then and there. Now they are not the only ones to know the answer to that question, but other people can also benefit from their question as well. Customers will often leave you a "heart," which represents a like, whenever their question is answered. Before the Question and Answer session, you can make a post letting your customers and partner businesses know about the time and date that you will be doing it on. Instagram Live (unlike Snapchat stories or Instagram stories) do not have a minimum or maximum time limit put on it. This means that the session can last as long as you want it to. On top of it, there is a record of every person who watched your video. This way you know who is really interested in your business and/or the products that you are selling. This can help you better figure out what kind of person to advertise to and keep track of loyal customers.

How-To Sessions and Other Tutorials for Cooking Businesses, Tutoring Businesses, Sports Coaches, Music Teachers, etc - Capturing Your Work in Action!

This one is mainly for people that are offering services rather than a product. Often times, before people choose one person that offers a service, they shop around first to see who is the best at what they are offering. Show your customers what you've got! Make them fall so in love with the way you do things that they throw cash at your door so that you can teach them how to do things.

For example, if you coach club soccer, you can stream a video of practice and let all the mothers watch how you teach children before they decide to enroll in your program for the year. If you are a makeup artist at Sephora, you can film a customer (with their permission) and show everyone else what you can do. If you do a good job, girls will be flocking at your door to do makeup for their wedding, prom, or other special occasions. If you own a cooking business and would like to host a special video to show customers how to make one specific item, you can Livestream your cooking process. If you have a teaching or tutoring job, you could stream a video of you teaching a class so that people can see your style and figure out for themselves if they like the way you teach. This gives people a personal feel to your services even if they are not there with you.

In order to do this, you would need something to hold your phone in place, like a phone stand or a small tripod. However, there are many benefits to this even though you do probably have to buy a tripod. People know what exactly they are getting into, so they are more inclined to pick you over someone else they know nothing about!

Introduce a New Product Through Instagram Live!

Customers do not always notice new products, even if you put them in the store. However, most people do check the internet every single day. With Instagram Live notifying every follower that you are now online, it is so easy to tell people all the details about a product that they might have otherwise never known about. The comment function will allow interested people to ask anything they want to about your product, and you can present it in the best light possible! This may also get people in the community talking about your product, and it is no less effective than any commercial that you see on TV! You can even give your phone number and let them buy the product right then and there from you, or you can link it to an online website that will allow them to place orders. that is if you are able to ship packages to their house. If not, they can always pick it up in store. If you're selling toys, go ahead and show people all its new features! If you're selling makeup, find a model and apply that lipstick on her! Once people see the product in use, they will be more than head over heels for it!

Discounts, Discounts, Discounts! How You Can Use People's Love for Cheap Stuff And Turn It into Profit!

Spend fifty dollars in a store and get ten dollars off! Who buys a whole bunch of stuff they are probably never even going to use when there is a coupon involved? Let's face it, everyone does! With Instagram Live, you can occasionally offer your customers a coupon code that they can only get when they watch your live story. When people hear about this (and don't know when the next coupon code will be given), they will watch your story every time that you go live! This gives you the opportunity to attract more viewers on your story, thus increasing your publicity.

"It's The Hard Knock Life for Us" - Show Your Customers Your Everyday Job - Make Your Business More Approachable!

Do you ever wonder about what a business does behind the scenes? Customers never really stop wondering about the process it takes for their products to be made. This is why you can use this to attract them to your Instagram story! It is always interesting to get to know the people that run a business! This is like a meet and greet at a concert - make your business look fun and approachable, and let people figure out what you do daily! When you do this, customers are more likely to see you as a friendly business than a place that is just out to get their money. This is a very humbling experience, and you do not even have to worry about your information leaking out because this is live and not recorded at all! Who knows, people may like the way you run your business so much that they want to become your future employee! You really never know.

Remember that Instagram Live increases your visibility and publicity. With so many people knowing about your business, your profits are bound to go up if you just know how to use this correctly! Of course, however, if you prefer for an announcement to be out for more than just one hour of live streaming, you may want to consider Instagram Stories instead.

Instagram Stories: A Twenty-Four Hour Advertisement

What if you wanted to post something on your feed but didn't feel like it was important enough? Instagram recognized this problem, so they created a function called the Instagram Stories. This feature was added to Instagram back in 2016. This makes Instagram similar to a competitor social media app, Snapchat. If there is something that you would like to share, but you do not feel like it is notable enough to be a post in itself, a story post is your perfect option.

How It Works

The videos you post can be up to fifteen seconds long, but they can be shorter if you want them to be. You can post as many photos or videos as you want. Whatever you post is up for twenty-four hours. If you don't feel like the raw video or photo is interesting enough, you can add filters and stickers on it, as well as text, emojis, or things you draw. Whatever you post will be at the top bar of everyone else's Instagram app, and they can view it if they want to or choose to ignore it if they do not want to. Even in the first six months of Instagram Stories' release, one hundred and fifty million people had already used it. It has been growing in popularity, perhaps even surpassing Snapchat's beginning stages.

How Can I Post a Story?

Here is how you post an Instagram story. Go to Instagram and swipe right once you get to your home page. Here, you will access the Instagram stories camera. You can post a normal picture of a product to advertise it, or you can go to "Boomerang" and it will post your picture in small snippets with a staggered effect if you want a dramatic look. There is also a rewind button if you want to play a video backward for fun, and a hands-free video recording option. Once you are done, you can press next and send it to your story, and ta-da, it is done. You can also turn the flash off if you are taking a picture of technology or in the bright daylight. Even if you don't like the post, you can press the X button and start all over.

- Filters: You can swipe right after you have taken the picture to add a filter. These often polish up your picture and if it is a picture of your employees, they would probably appreciate it!

- Art and Drawing Options: In order to draw on your picture or add some sort of comment with your own handwriting, you can click on the icon that looks like a pen on the top right corner of the page. Once you are there, you can select any color and decide on what you want.

- Adding Fonts or Text: Press the Aa button, then you can add a little mini caption right on your picture! You can move it around the picture as well.

- Stickers: There are so many Instagram stickers for you to choose from! There are more than just the traditional emojis at your disposal. There are random stickers about your location, the time, and more.

- In the future, you will be able to add a LINK to the picture on your story! For now, that is still in beta testing and only available to specific accounts.

Instagram stories can be used for the same things that the Live stories can be used for. It may be easier to start promotions or coupons through the stories since it is there for twenty-four hours.

Now you know a lot of the basics you need to interact with your customers online. With the right people managing your Instagram account, you can appear as an approachable and friendly business and promote whatever new products, services, or deals that you have going on right now. However, even with all the amazing benefits of natural marketing online, sometimes you still need paid advertisements to get your business out in the first place. The next chapter will show you how to navigate the world of Instagram's paid advertisements, tell you about how much they cost, show you their benefits, and reveal the different types of advertisements that you can create.

Chapter 3:

Paid Advertisements: When a Little Cash Spent Turns into a Lot of Cash in Your Pocket

Instagram offers a whole new world of advertising through its paid options. The good news about paid advertisements is that every single ad blends right in with the rest of the person's visible "news feed," making it hard to ignore when it seems like a regular post. In addition, Instagram is pretty smart. Once you pay for an ad, it makes sure that your ads are reaching your "target audience," or the types of people that you want it to reach (to maximize the profit of your business, of course!).

There is nothing that you want to spend money on more than an Instagram ad. People rarely read newspapers or magazines anymore, and many people go on the Internet to shop for whatever they need. This makes it easy to advertise on social media, which is still often cheaper than actual advertisements in the paper. The truth is that if you want to spend money on any social media website, it is best for you to spend it on Instagram. Research has shown that it has the most active community, surpassing both Facebook and Twitter.

However, you have to remember that Facebook bought Instagram about five years ago, so every Instagram ad has to run through Facebook's Ad Manager. Luckily for you, Facebook Ad Manager is a very simple process, and it takes only about a few minutes to start up an ad.

There are so many different types of advertisements that I am going to introduce you to before I show you how to activate them!

1) Photo Ads: These advertisements are promoted with both a description and any sort of artsy/edited or natural picture of your choice. These are the most basic types of advertisements, and you can create one through any photo editing app or camera app there is.

2) Video Ads: You can create up to a sixty-second video to display as an advertisement. It will blend in with all of the other posts (that they follow) that the person sees. These videos can also be accompanied by sound, so you can describe a product in full or ask your followers for advice on how to improve your company.

3) Carousel Ads: Is one picture not enough for you to describe your company's goals and objectives or to promote your current deal? Create a carousel ad to where you can post up to ten pictures in one post! This way, you can promote various products or show different aspects of your company! It is better to pick the Carousel Ad anyway just because it allows you to post multiple pictures. This helps you get the biggest deal out of what you pay for!

4) Story Ads: These are very similar to Snapchat's stories. When browsing through your friends' stories, you may

sometimes see a "Sponsored" story that seems to appear out of nowhere. These are paid story advertisements, and you can create one for your business too. This way, everyone gets to see your advertisement before they get to see their friend's story.

How to Create an Instagram Ad

First of all, you need to create a Facebook Page. This can be done through your personal Facebook account, and this page will be linked to your Instagram business account. It is hard to give you a definite price that your ad will cost because it depends on the end goals of your ad and who you want to target it to.

There are two mainstream ways that people mainly use to start creating ads on Instagram.

- The Ads Manager (on Facebook). This is a step by step guide through Facebook that helps you create an ad. For one, it will ask you about your "marketing objective." You can decide if you want to spread the name of your brand around or simply let the ad "reach" new people that have not seen it before. Next up, you will need to decide the main goal of this ad and beyond that. Do you want people to go to a different link, not on Instagram (like a website to buy things)? In that case, select the Traffic ad. You can also target the ad to where you will get more people talking about the product through comments, likes, and shares. that's called Engagement, so if you want that, select the Engagement ad. There are many more options, but once you have selected yours, it is time to start on your ad! They will ask you for some information, including where you live, the money you use, and the time zone that you are in. This is so that they can better tailor your ads to the right audience. Speaking of your audience, the next step you take is selecting your audience. You can target the location, ages, and gender that you want to see your ad. You can also choose to only tailor the ad to people who speak English if all you speak is English. Perhaps the most useful tool for this Ads Manager is the "Detailed Targeting" function. Here, you can tailor the ad to anyone with a specific interest. For example, McDonald's would tailor their ads to "fast food lovers" or "french fry lovers." You can also send the ad to people who like a specific another page. This gives you the edge over your competitors because if you're another local coffee shop, you can promote your ad to everyone else in the area who liked Starbucks' Instagram profile. The important part comes next. You have to set your budget now. For instance, you can set a daily budget of ten dollars so that your company will never spend more than ten dollars a day on an advertisement. This helps you save money and get your business out there at the same time by finding the most efficient way to start a business. After this, you connect both your Instagram account and your Facebook page, and then you are done! Your ad is up and running, and people will start finding your business in no time!

- The Power Editor: This option is also on Facebook, and it is also fairly easy to use. Once you get to the Power Editor, press "Create Campaign." You enter in your information, and it basically takes you back to the Ads Manager. You then enter in all your information and budget, just like you would in the regular Ads Manager.

Most people only use the Power Editor to manage several different ads at once.

Tips to Make the Most Out of Different Types of Advertisements

1) For photo ads, make sure that you are keeping it simple and to the point. In a picture, there is not much room to express your message, so less is more. Add stickers, writing, and text, but do not make it so big and distracting that it takes away from your product.

2) Put a link on your advertisement, and link it straight to your online website that your company may have. Go to your ad and press "Promote," and pay to put the website link on the ad. This allows people to go straight to that page to buy your product if they like it.

3) Use carousel ads to tell a story. Keep it interesting. No one wants to hear about a cleaning tool and what it looks like, but if you tell a story about how a single mom of three kids used that to simplify her busy schedule, all of the sudden, people sympathize with her and pay more attention to your product.

4) People will scroll past your ad if it is a blatant ad, similar to how we all hang up on a call that is blatantly selling something. Integrate your ad into people's Instagram feeds and make it blend in.

5) Keep your ads consistent and make them look similar. It helps add to your brand name if people can spot a picture and know it is from your company.

6) Use Instagram Video. Not many people have the time and patience to create a video. that makes videos stand out from thousands of pictures that people scroll past every single day. Videos are also useful - if you are going to spend money on an ad, you might as well show your customers what your product can do. Put that electric bike to the test and capture a bunch of models having fun in your brand's bikini. When people see that other people are having a good time with your product, they are way more inclined to buy it!

7) Add A Call To Action! - Call To Action is a simple trick that you can add to your advertisement that makes the customers able to press one button and go straight to a website or an app downloading page. You don't have to tell people to go to the link in your biography for a promotion. Set up a call to action and one simple button will take them to a link!

8) Use Hashtags! You need to use hashtags in advertisements too, not just regular posts. This way, people are reminded of your brand name's hashtag or can find you through a common hashtag. It never hurts to include one!

Chapter 4:

Photo and Video Magic! How to Sell Your Product Just Through the Superpower of Editing

Let's face it. Just like no one likes looking at an ugly stripper, no one likes looking at an advertisement that is bland and not unique at all. Part of selling your product is packaging it right; part of having an ad succeed on Instagram is making it right. This is why photo and video editing becomes so important in today's technological age. If it doesn't look good, many customers will not even give your product a chance before they condemn it to hell. This chapter will show you the basics of video and photo editing through a few free and popular apps, helping you make your product look as neat as possible. Once you know how to sell your product, people will constantly be signing up to get it.

There are many apps out there that can help you edit a photo. Of course, you don't want to edit it to the point where people do not recognize the model wearing your clothing or your product in itself. However, the right edits can make your products look higher class.

We'll start with VSCO, the most popular photo editing app in the Instagram community. This app is available through both the Apple Store and Google Play Market. The best part about it is that it is completely free for you to use! Though some may see this app as a photo blog only, it has many photo editing options that can help your product or service have the professional look to it. You do not even need to touch the blog part of it at all. When you first open the app, sign up for an account to access all the tools. Then, a screen with a plus sign should pop up. Press the plus sign to import your photo, and you can edit it from there. Once your photo is uploaded, select it and then press the button with two lines on the bottom left-hand corner. This starts your editing process.

- FILTERS: These are especially useful if you are promoting a fashion business (such as modeling) or a travel business that requires you to take scenic pictures of the world. When you first load up the picture in the editor, this is the first function that it will take you to. You should select one that works, then click on it. You then get to pick the intensity of the picture. The left circles mean that the filter is weaker, and the right circles show that the filter is stronger. Take your pick. There is a free set available on VSCO, but you have to pay if you want the others.

- BRIGHTNESS AND CONTRAST: Press the button with two lines again, and click on Contrast. This will allow you to change how light some parts of the picture are and vice versa. You want to increase this if you want your center product to stand out from its background.

- EXPOSURE: This one is basically adding a white light/sunlight to a picture. This might be needed if you are taking a picture of the sunny beach and would like a more dramatic effect.When you're done, press the check mark and go to the next function.

- STRAIGHTEN: You can adjust the picture if you took it at a slightly altered angle, you can get it fixed right away. that way, your product is at the center, and there will be nothing to distract the viewer from it! Simply move the bar from left to right to straighten your picture.

- HORIZONTAL/VERTICAL PERSPECTIVE: This is similar to the straightening tool. It focuses on the angle you took the picture at.

- CROP: This is oh so important for photo advertisements! You can use this to crop photos to Instagram size. Though Instagram tends to take advertisements of many different crops, it is best to use the traditional one to one dimension!

- CLARITY, SHARPEN, and SATURATION TOOLS: These all help add color and make your ad clearer than it could have been.

- VIGNETTE: These will help add drama to your travel photos if you are in that business, or perhaps a picture of a fancy restaurant or modeling service as well. Use this to your advantage because it adds a tiny dark border to the picture. This causes you to focus on the center object.

The rest of the VSCO tools are not really that relevant to photo advertisement editing, but keep these tools in mind and you are probably set. You do not want to edit the photo so much that it looks completely fake and like the opposite of what you are selling, but these tools can help enhance your product just enough to where someone who was just thinking about purchasing your product or service might just go ahead and buy it.

There is also another app that you can use. Although it costs around four dollars, this app allows you to edit your pictures and place text on it as well. The good news is that it goes ahead and places the text for you in an artsy manner, and you do not have to spend much time editing the photo. This app is called "Over," and it is available for both Android and the iPhone. This is mainly a typography or text editor app, but it may come in handy if you are trying to design a paid advertisement.

If you prefer a simple app that concentrates more on brightness and contrast, you may prefer an app called Afterlight. This is available on iOS, Android, and Windows. This app allows you to change the color, saturation, and angle of the picture really well. It only costs ninety-nine cents.

Having a Consistent Style on Instagram for Your Business

Though it is fun to experiment with various different filters and different fonts, it can get a bit inconsistent if you are trying to build up the name of a brand. People will find your posts hard to recognize in a crowd, and they will not be as memorable if you just edit whatever you want. To have a certain signature look, you have to design your Instagram feed like you would design a room in your house. Everything should look neat and have a certain style to it. The good news is that you get to pick your style!

First of all, you should decide on a specific "tone" or "feeling" of the whole page. Do you want it to be lighthearted or darker?

This really should depend on the type of product you sell. For instance, if you are a makeup and beauty product store, you probably should not have a page that gives off an eerie vibe like a haunted house.

Next, you need to decide on a few signature filters that you will use for your business. This doesn't mean that you need to choose just one, but it is probably best if every single one of your posts is polished with one out of five filters to keep it simple and memorable. If you want to, you could also ditch the filter altogether and go with a natural look of the photo.

With text, you could create a company watermark if you would like. If that is way too much trouble for you, you could consider keeping all your fonts on posts the same two or three signature fonts so that your posts still maintain a unique look.

Finally, you should decide on a color scheme. Ideally, it should be your company's colors, but try to keep this consistent. This way, if anyone sees those few colors put together, they are automatically reminded of your particular product and company. The idea is not to have so much fun with editing that you do not keep a recognizable style!

Adobe Photoshop Basics

Sometimes, a phone editor is simply not enough, and you want to create a more artsy ad for a special product or event. Adobe Photoshop is the premier program for photo editing if you want to create the prettiest ads. The downside is that the program is expensive, but if your business can afford it, this is a really good tool for creating advertisements. The program has a thirty-day free trial if you are only interested in making a few official advertisement pictures and never want to touch the program again after that!

Here is how you use some of the basics located on the toolbar of Adobe Photoshop.

- MOVE TOOL (Press V on the Keyboard to activate it) - This tool looks like a compass and a little triangle. Click on it and you can drag anything on your screen and move it to another place.

- CROP TOOL (Press C on the Keyboard to activate it) - This icon looks like a square with edges not cut off with a slash right through it. You should just enter the dimensions you want once you press on this tool, and it will give it to you. This is helpful for making all your business advertisements perfect for Instagram and the right size!

- THE MAGIC WAND (Press W on the Keyboard to activate it) - This icon looks exactly like a wand. This removes anything around a spot with a similar color. This is helpful if you want to replace a color with another one or change the background on an image.

- CLONE STAMPS (Press S on the Keyboard to activate it!) - This looks exactly like it sounds. It is a stamp icon. This is what you can do to cut someone out of a picture (like a photobomber who interferes with a picture of your product). It takes the background around it and makes one area of the picture blend right in with the background.

- PAINTBRUSH AND THE PENCIL OPTION (Press B on the Keyboard to activate it!) - Th

- ERASER (Press E on the Keyboard to activate it!) - This is pretty self-explanatory. You move your mouse over whatever you want to get rid of and it's gone.

- PAINT CAN (Press G on the Keyboard to activate it!) - This icon looks exactly like a spilled can of paint. You can use this to fill in backgrounds with either a solid color or a gradient (like going from white to green or going from blue to purple, etc).

- TYPE TOOL (Press T on the Keyboard to activate it!) - For business people like you, this may be the most important tool that you can use on an advertisement. This tool looks like a giant T on the toolbar. You can select whatever font you want, whatever size you want, and rotate it however you please. This is really useful if you want to put the name of your business, product, or the promotion onto your picture itself instead of putting it in a caption that people might not even read.

- SHAPE TOOL (Press U on the Keyboard to activate it!) - This lets you create geometric shapes to design your ad with. It looks like a rectangle on the toolbar.

- LASSO TOOL (Press L on the Keyboard to activate it!) - This icon looks like a small paper origami bird trying to fly up. The lasso lets you "mask," or select an oddly shaped item and drag it out of the picture by simply selecting around its corners. This one is harder to use but very rewarding if you know how to use it the right way.

- HAND TOOL (Press H on the Keyboard to activate it!) - It's sad to say that something this simple might be the most useful tool in all of the Photoshop. It is shaped exactly like it sounds - it looks like a giant Mickey Mouse hand. You can use this tool to go back to anything you did and drag it out of the picture if you do not like where it is placed. You can move things around with this.

- ZOOM TOOL (Press Z on the Keyboard to activate it!) - The zoom tool looks like a magnifying glass. It lets you view the small things in the middle. You can use this to edit the finest details of a picture.

There are many other tools on Photoshop and it takes years to master, but if you know these tools you should be set on making a simple advertisement.

Finally, there is one more trick to working with Instagram. Now that pictures can zoom, a picture of your product can look really cool if you have to zoom in to see what it really looks like. This is different from how many people post and elicits attention if you know how to do it right.

Now that you know how to make your advertisements pretty and packaged, you need to know when exactly you need to post your pictures that you worked so hard to edit!

Chapter 5:

Timing, Location, and Demographics! Target the Right People and You're Set

When should I post? Will the people around me know that I posted? When are people actually looking at their social media apps? Am I just being annoying and posting way too much? These are all questions that need to be answered in order to know when exactly to post to make the most out of your marketing/campaigning.

First of all, you need to know how to track how well your posts have been doing. Once you open up Instagram, press the fifth button (the furthest one to the right) on the bottom toolbar. This leads you to your profile. You will need to click on that then look at the top toolbar where your username is. Beside your username, there should be a few bars (an icon that looks like a bar graph). Press that. This is your "Instagram Insights" button, and it will tell you a lot of information about your followers and engagement. It will show you how well your posts and stories are doing, and what kind of person (gender, age, location) most prefers them. This will help you decide who to target your advertising and products towards next time. You will get to see your impressions, which is the number of people that have viewed your posts, even if they have done nothing.

Honestly though, it is not enough to know only the demographics of your followers. You might not know this, but you can also use your own geographic location to boost sales and gain publicity on Instagram.

The World of Geotagging

Every phone has a tracker in it. No, it's not some ploy by the government. Rather, it is a GPS chip that helps you navigate the world you live in. Because of this, "geo tagging" your posts on Instagram is easy. Geotagging is basically the fancy term used for sharing your location with someone (your latitude and longitude coordinates on a map). Don't worry about accidentally leaking your location, because Instagram will not share it with your post unless you instruct it to.

So how exactly do you add a geotag to a post? Believe it or not, it is actually fairly simple. When you upload a photo, you can instantly press "Add Location" on there and select a city or a place. Your location will appear as text underneath your username on your actual post.

This comes in convenient because you can click on that location and instantly be directed to all the different posts that have ever been taken before at that location! It is an excellent tool.

Not to mention, you can list your business as one of the location tags. When pressing "Add Location," just select the custom location button and add your store to the Instagram database. This way, everyone who has ever been at your store can tag the pictures of themselves in your store or the picture of all the products they get and share it with their followers! Any frequent customer who clicks the business location geotag might be able to see your newest products and sales, and anybody who does not know anything about your business will now know what you offer! If you have a special event and customers geotag it, they may attract new customers who show up at your front door!

Creating a geotag is the first thing you can do for your business if you want your customers to start posting about the products that they get.

How Often Do I Post, and When Should I Post to Reach the Most People?

You want to post just enough for people to remember that you exist, and you want to not post so much that you scare off all your potential customers because they think you are spamming.

If you post a picture of your newest product at two in the morning, you're not likely to get many views, likes, or comments in the few hours after you post it. Like a game of chess, posting things on Instagram requires strategy, and timing is one of those things you want to get right if you do not want to waste your time posting things that no one will see.

Unlike Facebook, Twitter, or even your own email, most people check Instagram many times a day. This app is easy to check throughout the day because a picture feed is easier to scroll through than one with a whole bunch of words. Nevertheless, there are still peak times.

According to a study conducted by SumAll, you should post around five to six in the afternoon on Mondays through

Fridays. This is when people normally get off work and go grab a bite to eat, so they often have time to grab out their phone and scroll past their Instagram feed.

Even with that information, it is good to remember that it is important for you to look at your posts and see when your own followers and community get on Instagram. When you go to the "Instagram Insights" button, you can see when people are commenting on and liking your posts. You may want to cater to your own clientele once you have an established community who supports your small business.

Another thing that you should remember with posting is consistency. No one wants to follow a business account that does not post very often, no matter how good your business is. No one will remember your account if you only post once a month. In fact, according to blogs on Bufferapp, Union Metrics noted that the businesses who posted around one or two times a day attracted the most audience on their posts and had the most people interacting with them.

Does Posting Pictures of People Increase My Engagement?

Yes! All businesses should post pictures of their customers or employees if they are able to. Research has shown that posting pictures of people helps attract more likes and comments than if you didn't.

How Do I Write Captions that Do Not Annoy People?

Captions are one of the most tricky things about Instagram. You should limit the caption to about three readable lines because after you post more than 2200 characters, Instagram no longer shows your full caption. The best captions have about three hashtags and say something witty about the product. that way, people will remember.

Target Younger Audiences

This is especially helpful if you are a business that mainly serves young people. Most Instagram users are young adults around the ages of 18-30. You should remember this when you create your advertisements and decide if you want to invest so much on Instagram advertising or not.

Chapter 6:

Come to Win! Cool Contests that Help You Make It Big Once You're All Set Up

If someone gave you a chocolate bar (or your favorite food) and said that you could have it if you just did one jumping jack, would you do it? Yeah, I bet you would. Let's face it, people like free stuff, even if they have to do something stupid to get it. Above that, people like to win. This is why having contests as a business account is such a necessity. According to a study by Tailwind, a company associated with Instagram, ninety-one percent of posts with over a thousand comments have to do with some sort of contest. These might be a little bit time consuming, but they are actually your best bet to marketing!

We discussed some of this in Chapter 2, but there are actually a variety of contests that can help your business grow even bigger. Contests help you interact with your customers. They help you advertise through your treasured customers. It keeps your own community engaged and also helps spread the word to people who may not have tried your product or service before. You do not even have to spend that much on the reward. Often times, even the smallest rewards will attract people. Your best bet is going with store credit because that means that the money comes back to you anyway (if you are a business that sells products).

1) Upload Your Own Photo Contests - This is the biggest gimmick that you can use to make your customers advertise for you. If you are a travel agency, you can have people upload the wildest adventures that they have ever been on for a chance to win a $100 voucher to one of your tours. Hey, that also means that they have to spend whatever the difference is in your company - not your competitor's. If you are an Italian restaurant, you can have people upload the happiest memories they have eating pizza for a chance to win free pizza at your store for a month. Although you do lose some initial supplies and/or money, you will likely gain a long term customer. Not to mention, a lot of people will know about your business if you are just getting started out if there is a promotion going around.

2) "Like To Win!" Lotteries - This one depends on chance, but it gets a lot of people to like your post, which causes it to be shown a lot on their friends' "Explore" page. You can create a campaign to where people have to "like" your picture to enter a contest. Then, you get to draw a person out of a jar as a winner and offer them something. It's best if you give them a product that your company is selling, as this not only promotes your social media page but also your product as well.

3) "Fill In The Blank," Guessing, or Commenting Contests - You can see who knows more about your product or a company by hosting one of these contests. Perhaps you can reward those that answer the question right with a coupon code, or you could feature their profile on your

business page. Either way, it is a fun little way to get the community engaged.

4) "Tag A Friend" Giveaways - This is the easiest way to get people who have not even heard of your brand to try a product. You simply tell someone to post a picture in your product or with your product (depending on if it is a food item, clothing item, or collector's merchandise). After they post it, they should tag a friend in the post and then follow the store account. that automatically qualifies them to be entered in the contest, and you can select a winner through a random drawing.

5) In Store Picture or "Selfie" Contests - This works best if you actually have a storefront that sells products. Have people take pictures going to your store and then upload it online with a hashtag for their chance to win something. This not only entices the person to come to your store, but it also causes them to shamelessly advertise for your business on the internet. that will only help your business in the long run, even if you do give away a measly product. You can also feature your customers on your business page so that they know they are appreciated! The more a customer likes the management of a business, the more likely they are to come back, even if your product is not better than your competitor's.

Instagram contests take time to manage, and they can be a headache. However, it is the easiest way by far to reach everyone that you may want to connect with as a small business. Now that you know how to start a business account on Instagram and have everything set up, that is the best way you can continue to grow your customer base and increase in popularity as a product. Do not forget to associate each contest with a unique hashtag, or else you will be finding it difficult to keep track of everything on the post.

How Do You Host a Good Contest? Here Are Some Tips.

1. Make sure the rules are clear so that there is no dispute in who won or how to enter the contest! It is the worst thing that can happen if two people start arguing. It makes you look unorganized as a business, and you may have to give out two prizes instead if you cannot figure out who actually won.

2. Make a web page for the contest if it is big enough so people can make submissions there.

3. Don't make your contest last longer than a month! It can get tiring, and you might be too lazy to organize it by then. People may also forget about it, and the contest loses its purpose of getting your name out there.

The most important thing about any contest is that you need to keep it fun and interesting!

Now that you know how to manage these contests, you basically know everything you need to know to kick start your Instagram business today! If we could sum it all up, we would say that you need to separate your business account from your personal account to keep it professional. You need a distinct style for your brand and witty captions and posts that describe your product! Your information has to be correct, and don't forget to use hashtags and interact with your customers! Make sure you know who your audience is so that you can target them and others who are interested in the same stuff as them!

Keep track of how you are doing through your Instagram Insights button, and create a location for yourself on the Instagram map! Once you do all of these things, you can start having live videos of everything that goes on in your business, answering all of your customers' important questions!

We hope that you have found this book useful. Even when you make it up there as a high earning business that attracts a lot of customers, these tips will still help you further advertise to even more people! Today's technology age makes it easy for you to advertise, and you might not even have to spend as much! Go get started on Instagram today; it is only one app download away.

Conclusion

Thank for finishing this book all the way to the end of *Instagram Marketing: A Picture Perfect Way to Strike It Rich!* We'd like to also thank Instagram for providing such a great social networking platform, so awesome that we were able to write a book about all the little marketing tricks that we can use through that app! We hope that we gave you enough information (and more) to make your business the next big hit on the Internet! Remember that our tips are not the only ways out there that you can use to show off your business to everyone else. Continue learning about online marketing, for it is for sure in the future of every businessman's life. You have the edge over your competitors now that you know all the tips in this book.

Now, get your nose out of this book! Your job now is to follow the steps in this book and apply it to your business now, or perhaps even start a new one and market through Instagram! Team up with other businesses and let your whole town (and people further than that) know that you have something great to offer! There is no reason to wait - the earlier you start this, the more people know about what you have to sell, and the more money will come your way!

If you feel overwhelmed or bogged down by all the stresses of your business already, consider delegating some work time to advertise on the Internet. Get this account set up during work hours by asking your employees to help you! If it can increase the number of people interested in your business, the one extra day of work will have been well worth it!

We wish you nothing but the best of luck in all your endeavors! We believe in you, and we know that you will make it big! If you succeed, that means we have succeeded as well in writing this book.

Finally, we would really appreciate it if you leave a review on Kindle! A lot of work was invested into this book so that you can take our tips and make it rich! Any comments are helpful for us, and we hope that this book was exactly what you needed to kick start your business online.

Check Out My Other Books

Below you'll find some of my other popular books that are popular on Amazon and Kindle as well. Simply click on the links below to check them out. Alternatively, you can visit my author page on Amazon to see other work done by me.

www.ingramcontent.com/pod-product-compliance
Lightning Source LLC
Chambersburg PA
CBHW071216210326
41597CB00016B/1836